4 Sara Cook

12 Gina Ferrari

20 Jessica Grady

30 Nikki Parmenter

36 Kate Wells

BOOK SIX

WOWbook

Guest Editor
Lynda Monk

6

Q&A 44 LYNDA MONK & CHRISTINE CHESTER

2020 LOCKDOWN 56 ISOLATION STORIES

64 ARTISTS' PROFILES

Welcome *to* WOWbook ⑥

BOOK SIX

This is such an exciting issue with plenty of projects to keep you going through those dark evenings.

I love something new to put on my wall, and Gina Ferrari creates a stitched collage, perfect for displaying in your home.

Jessica Grady shows us another way to de-clutter by using 'waste' materials that everyone will have at home, to create some fabulous embellishments. From recycled plastic waste and metals to washers – all it takes is a bit of imagination.

I also love a bit of bling and Kate Wells certainly delivers with her workshop on how to create gold lace on dissolvable fabric.

We are going abroad now with Sara Cook who uses hand-dyed silk organza to demonstrate a decorative seam used in Korean textiles and Nikki Parmenter takes us to Holland for *Tulipmania*, showing us how to transform a drawing or photograph into a mixed media piece.

For the celebrity interview in this issue, I chose the amazing artist, Christine Chester. Christine has recently opened her new studio, Studio 11, in the centre of Eastbourne, West Sussex UK, and has shared with us a fascinating insight into her beginnings through to her present practice.

Finally, the elephant in the room, Covid-19. I think it's true to say that the pandemic has had an effect on all of us, especially creatively. However, the number of online workshops made available, many free and some being live via Zoom, all without having to leave home, were all welcomed as a way of keeping us sane.

Sue Brown, Louise Asher and Liske Johnson decided to start a project during lockdown to encourage creativity by asking people to make a small collagraph plate. They were then sent to Sue who printed them out and then posted them back, ready for stitch. These were then made into quilted hangings and you can see the results and their thought processes in *Same Sea, Different Boat*.

I must admit that one of the things I've missed the most is the annual shows, with the inspiration gained from the exhibiting artists, and learning about all the guilds and groups that are available to join – and perhaps more importantly, the opportunity to buy even more 'stuff'!

Enjoy!

Lynda Monk

ᐯ *Mustard Hill* by Jessica Grady. This is a three-dimensional sculpture, 14½in (36cm) in diameter, created using recycled coffee pods, hand-dyed aquarium tubing, old gift ribbon and sliced hair-curler sequins. Many of the embellishments, including the tough plastics, were carefully drilled and embellished by hand before stitching onto the fabric base. *Mustard Hill* was part of a collection of six sculptures for an exhibition entitled 'Wild With Art Textiles Made in Britain'.

∧ One of Gina Ferrari's
  unique painted and
  stitched collages, perfect
  to hang on your wall.

WRAPPING UP WITH BOJAGI
Make a **Summer Glow** *wallhanging*

∨ *Summer Glow* wallhanging inspired by the heat of summer in my garden and created with hand-dyed silk organza, pieced together with *kkekki* seams.

Sara Cook

The hot colours in this wallhanging are inspired by the heat of summer in the garden. I like to hand-dye my silk organza to get the colours that I want but you can buy commercially dyed silk organza from specialist suppliers.

In this workshop, you will learn how to cut and piece silk organza using the unique seaming technique in Korean textiles known as a *kkekki* seam, where the seam is stitched three times and folded twice.

What are *bojagi*?

Bojagi (formerly Romanised as *pojagi*) translates as 'wrapping cloth' and is the generic name given to this type of stitched textile. Most of the surviving examples of *bojagi* date to the Joseon Dynasty (1392–1910) but some can be dated as far back as the Three Kingdoms period (57 BCE–668 CE).

Bojagi have played an important role in traditional Korean culture and have been used regularly to wrap, carry and store objects. Until the 1950s they were used to wrap or cover everything from bedding and clothes to food dishes and for religious rituals. These functional domestic items were not made as a hobby but were produced along with clothing and bedding items essential in the household. They were an integral part of daily living.

Some were pieced together creating colourful geometric designs using leftover household fabrics whilst others were made from a single piece of cloth; others were heavily embroidered.

Most pieces were square and came in different sizes depending upon their use – usually around 1pok (35cm) to 10pok (350cm). Some had long ties attached to their corners whilst others were lined with oiled paper for use as food coverings with handles made of folded fabric. They served a practical need, were beautifully made and were often imbued with symbols for good luck, health and wealth, and they seem to have had a significance for the maker beyond their practical use. A wrapping cloth can take a simple form but convey a profound message through the use of colour and symbolism.

Bojagi were used by all members of society and could be folded and stored, taking up minimal space in smaller homes. Their uses give us a glimpse into past lifestyles and ritual practices.

In an average household, the living space often doubled-up as a sleeping area and as a place to eat. Quilted sleeping mats would be folded away and wrapped. Wardrobes and chests of drawers were not common, so clothing and special items were contained and protected by wrapping cloths.

During the Chosen period, Confucian philosophy gradually dominated state ideology and the impact on women's social status was such that by the 16th century, women's lives were largely confined to their role as wives. In wealthy and middle-class homes, men and women lived in separate living quarters, the kitchen being in the women's quarters. Women were excluded from any formal education and lived very restricted lives. One way they could express themselves creatively was in making bojagi. This isolation seems to have contributed to the very special work that was created. No records or images survive of patterns that may have been followed but there are some surviving Chosen dynasty court records listing vast numbers of bojagi that were used and needed for various ceremonial functions.

The bojagi could be made from ramie, hemp, cotton or silk. Perhaps the most appealing are the jogakbo or pieced patchwork cloths made from small scraps, in which recycled leftover pieces of fabric were made into abstract patchwork designs.

∨ This traditional jogakbo (pieced) covering cloth is a copy of one in the British Museum's collection, c.1900–50. It is made from silk and pieced by hand using the seaming technique known as garumsol, which is joined using whip stitch. The handle is held in place with two bakgi mae dub or bat knots and the border is secured with rows of settam sangchim (triple stitch).

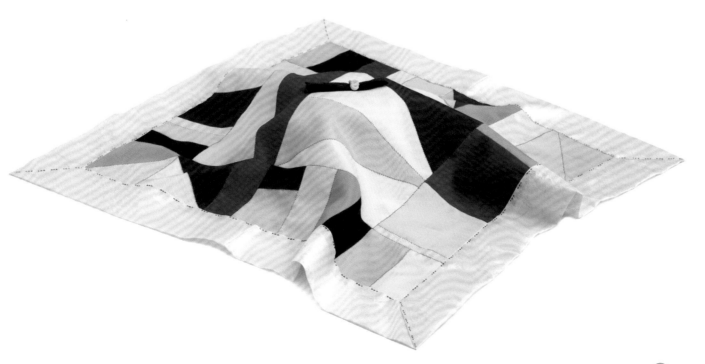

MATERIALS AND EQUIPMENT

- Three fat quarters of silk organza in a range of colours – yellow to orange shown here
- Three fat quarters of silk organza in a range of one colour (I have used pale to light cerise)
- 29½in (75cm) white silk organza
- Extra-fine pins
- Sewing machine
- 70 Microtex needle
- Toning thread
- Hera marker tool
- Pair of small sharp scissors
- Rotary cutter, mat and ruler

TIP
The silk organza should be well starched and pressed before you start sewing.

For this project, I suggest that you cut all your fabrics into strips before you start piecing. I like to clip them together into their different colours and hang them up.

By cutting each of the colours into similar widths, you should end up with a harmonious effect. If you prefer more contrast then you can vary the widths of the strips.

Workshop

It can be challenging to cut organza exactly on the straight of the grain. Starching the organza can help to stabilise it but it can still move around on the cutting mat. The best way to achieve an exact edge is to make a small snip in the edge of the fabric and to tear the fabric into strips. This is best done along the length of the fabric parallel to the selvedge.

1. Snip and tear each of the fabrics into 3in, 4in and 5in strips (8cm, 10cm and 13cm). Press the torn edges flat. Trim away the frayed edges with a rotary cutter (this needs to be set up on your cutting mat).

2. To begin, select two different-width strips. Pin these strips together along their length.

3. To make the *kkekki* seam, stitch with a scant ¼in (0.6cm) seam allowance along the length of the strips. My machine is a Bernina and I use my standard sewing machine foot, moving the needle to the first right-hand position. Reduce your stitch length to 2 – this stops the seams from unravelling. I use Aurifil 50 weight thread as this is a smooth two-ply thread but you can use a 60 weight thread as an alternative.

TIP
Use extra-fine pins when working with silk organza.

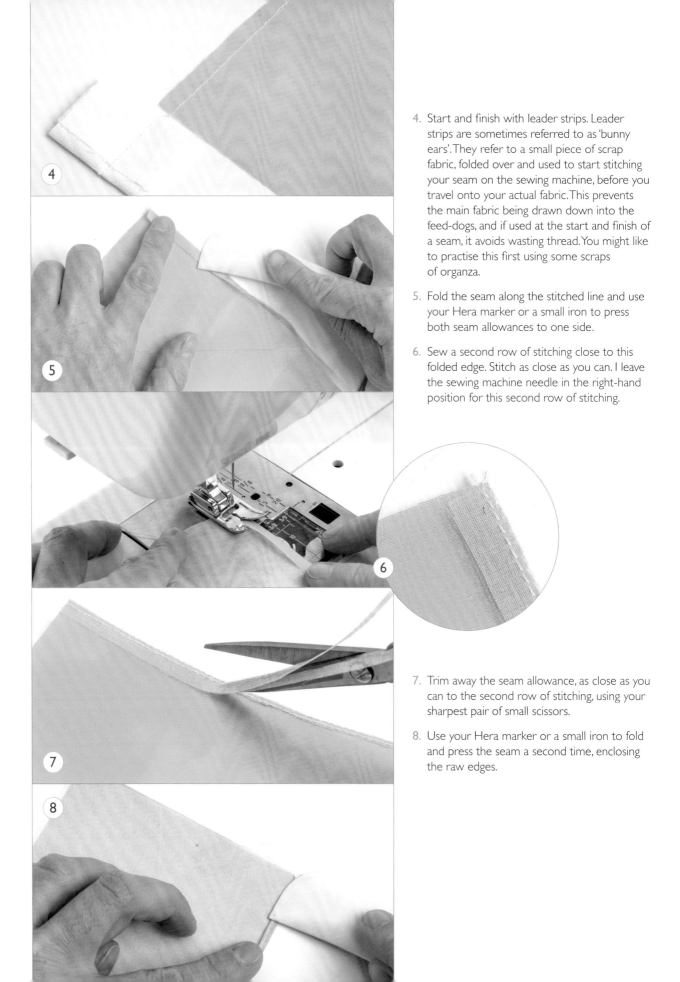

4. Start and finish with leader strips. Leader strips are sometimes referred to as 'bunny ears'. They refer to a small piece of scrap fabric, folded over and used to start stitching your seam on the sewing machine, before you travel onto your actual fabric. This prevents the main fabric being drawn down into the feed-dogs, and if used at the start and finish of a seam, it avoids wasting thread. You might like to practise this first using some scraps of organza.

5. Fold the seam along the stitched line and use your Hera marker or a small iron to press both seam allowances to one side.

6. Sew a second row of stitching close to this folded edge. Stitch as close as you can. I leave the sewing machine needle in the right-hand position for this second row of stitching.

7. Trim away the seam allowance, as close as you can to the second row of stitching, using your sharpest pair of small scissors.

8. Use your Hera marker or a small iron to fold and press the seam a second time, enclosing the raw edges.

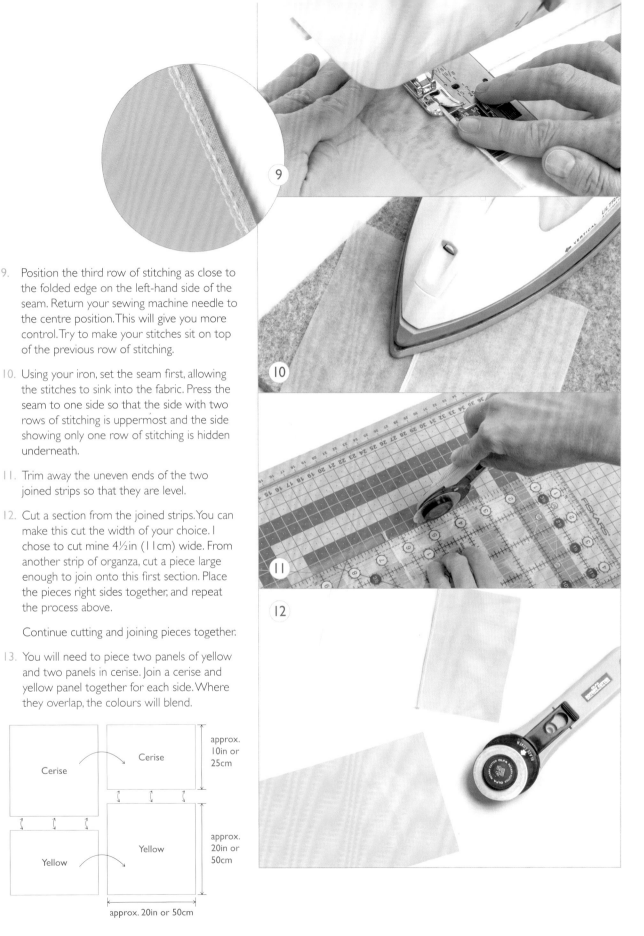

9. Position the third row of stitching as close to the folded edge on the left-hand side of the seam. Return your sewing machine needle to the centre position. This will give you more control. Try to make your stitches sit on top of the previous row of stitching.

10. Using your iron, set the seam first, allowing the stitches to sink into the fabric. Press the seam to one side so that the side with two rows of stitching is uppermost and the side showing only one row of stitching is hidden underneath.

11. Trim away the uneven ends of the two joined strips so that they are level.

12. Cut a section from the joined strips. You can make this cut the width of your choice. I chose to cut mine 4½in (11cm) wide. From another strip of organza, cut a piece large enough to join onto this first section. Place the pieces right sides together, and repeat the process above.

    Continue cutting and joining pieces together.

13. You will need to piece two panels of yellow and two panels in cerise. Join a cerise and yellow panel together for each side. Where they overlap, the colours will blend.

Cerise

Cerise

Yellow

Yellow

approx. 10in or 25cm

approx. 20in or 50cm

approx. 20in or 50cm

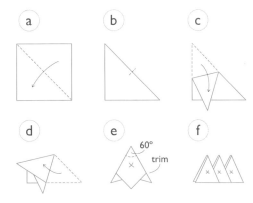

a   b   c

d   e   f

60°
trim
×

JakSsi (pine nut)

JakSsi are traditionally made from small squares of different-coloured fabric. They are often inserted into seams and as well as being symbols of good luck, they add an interesting textural effect. They appear to be very similar to prairie points, which are also made by folding and refolding a square of fabric to form a right-angle point. These decorative points, however, finish with either a 50° or 60° angle, depending upon which folding method you use.

1. First thread your needle with a single thread and put a knot on the end of it. Cut a 1¼in (3cm) square of organza.

2. Fold the square in half to form a rectangle. Fold the rectangle in half again and finger-crease the centre point. Using the centre mark, first fold one corner over, using the 60° angle line on your cutting mat or ruler as a guide. Finger-crease this in place. Now fold the other corner over. Even these folds out.

3. Stitch a temporary cross to hold the folded edges in place. Make sure this is towards the middle of the pine nut. You can trim away the uneven edges or leave them to be trimmed away once they have been set into the edge of the wallhanging. Use a pair of small scissors to trim away the uneven edges.

4. Make nine pine nut embellishments and then insert them into the outside edges of the wallhanging between two layers of fabric before turning the work out to the right side.

To finish

This type of work looks great hung in a window or against a plain wall. You could attach hanging loops to the top edge before you turn the work through or attach a fine fishing line to the corners and hang the work from this instead.

I hope you enjoy seeing the light passing through the layers.

> *Spring Green #1.* Inspired by new growth in spring. Hand-stitched with *homjil* (flat fell) seams made from silk and ramie fabric.

∧ My *Summer Glow* wallhanging.

> *Spring Green #1.* Detail. *JakSsi* pine nut decoration made from hand-dyed silk organza, added to the hanging before closing the outside edge.

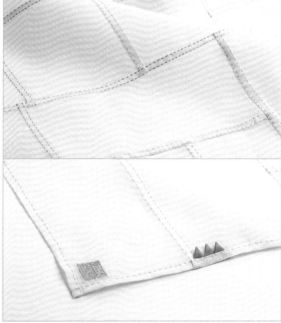

HOME IS WHERE THE ART IS
Creating a stitched collage

∧ My completed painted
and stitched collage.

Gina Ferrari

For the past twenty years or so I have taught machine embroidery and have created artwork using my machine as a drawing tool. Taking inspiration from many things – such as people, stories and the written word – I'm also inspired by the things seen on my daily dog walks. The trees, plants and birds viewed amid the changing seasons constantly inspire me and I'm always snapping pictures on my phone or making hasty sketchbook drawings (they have to be quick – my dog is easily distracted).

When we moved home last year, I was without a dedicated sewing space as most of my fabrics and threads were stashed away in boxes. I returned to my love of drawing and painting which I was able to do on a corner of the kitchen table. One day, when tearing up some paintings that hadn't worked and rearranging them in my sketchbook, I wondered if stitch could be added and, before I knew it, collaged and stitched pictures were being produced – these have inspired this workshop.

MATERIALS AND EQUIPMENT

- 2 or 3 sheets of watercolour or acrylic paper, A3 size, approx. 300gsm
- Acrylic paints in black, white and colours of your choice – I recommend two blues, two yellows and two reds in warm and cool tones
- Palette for mixing paint
- Acrylic inks (optional)
- Print roller/brayer
- Old plastic store or credit card
- Paintbrushes – a ¾in or 1in (2–2.5cm) flat brush was used for most of the work shown here
- Small piece of bubblewrap
- Scraps of thin collage papers, e.g. old book pages, maps, music manuscripts, tickets – you will not need much, but this adds texture
- Acrylic matte medium
- Paper scissors
- Glue stick
- Sewing machine set up for free machine embroidery
- Black sewing thread

∧ Another completed painted and stitched collage created with the method used in this workshop.

The painted papers used for the collage are built up with several layers of paint using different techniques. We begin by applying the first layer to a sheet of paper and, at the same time, create the background. A little about materials before you start …

I used acrylic paints and would definitely recommend them for this process rather than alternative media. They dry quickly, give a good coverage and you can easily build up layers of colour, both transparent and opaque. It's worth having some basic colours; the ones used in this workshop are my personal favourites, from which you can mix most other colours. Feel free to add any other colours that you like, but they are not necessary. It can also be fun to work with what you have and see what happens. Different colours will give different results.

My favourites are titanium white and Mars black – both are essential. I often use Payne's grey instead of black. The primary colours I prefer are cadmium yellow, yellow ochre, cadmium red light, magenta, cerulean blue and ultramarine. I also like to have a tube of cadmium orange, lime green and turquoise. Heavy body acrylics are used (as opposed to fluid) which are readily available both online and at any good art shop.

When painting I like to keep some spare sheets of paper beside me. After applying a colour, I scrape the excess paint from my brush, roller or card onto the spare sheet of paper, wiping off as much as possible on paper towels before washing my brush. There are a couple of reasons for doing this. As the paint builds up on the paper, you can get some interesting effects and colour combinations which can often be used as backgrounds for further work. I save them all! It also minimises the amount of paint that ends up down the drain. I wash my brushes in a large container rather than under a running tap and then filter the washing water before pouring it away (through a coffee filter paper). Acrylic paints are plastic and we don't want to be adding that to our oceans.

I also like to create drip effects with acrylic inks, but you can achieve similar effects with watered-down paint.

As acrylic paints dry quickly, it's useful to have a stay-wet palette, but you can easily make your own using an old kitchen tray. Onto that, put a couple of layers of kitchen towel, wetted thoroughly. On top of that, use a sheet of either tracing paper or baking parchment and you then have a palette that will keep your paints in a workable condition for at least twenty-four hours.

Now you are all set to create a painted and stitched collage.

Painting

1. For the first layer, squeeze some white paint plus a minuscule amount of black and blue paint onto one of the sheets of paper, and spread it over the surface using the roller. You are not aiming for an even coverage but a random light covering in neutral blue-grey colours. Add more paint as necessary to achieve the desired effect, then leave it to dry before adding the second layer.

2. Whilst you have these neutral colours on your roller, paint a second sheet of paper, paler than the first. Add more white paint if necessary. This will be your background sheet. Set it aside to dry. You will not be adding any more paint to this layer.

3. When the first sheet is dry, select three or four vibrant hot colours, such as pink, orange and yellow, and mix with a little white to create warm pastels. Apply these using an old store card or credit card, moving the paint around the surface, allowing some of the background to show. I also used some lime green for contrast. Although green is generally considered a cool colour, lime green has a high proportion of yellow so it's relatively warm. You can mix your own with a tiny amount of blue and quite a bit of yellow.

4. Once the layer of hot colours is dry, it's time to add some high-contrast areas of printing, using bubblewrap and the ends of cardboard tubes dipped in paint. Apply black paint sparingly to a piece of bubblewrap using a paintbrush, rather than dipping the bubblewrap in the paint. By using a brush, you can control the amount of paint on the bubblewrap, which gives a clearer print. Press the bubblewrap, paint side down, onto the surface of your painting to create printed areas. Repeat as often as you wish to create the desired effect. Still using the black paint, dip the end of a cardboard tube into the paint and use it to print circles. Allow to dry.

5. Repeat the printing process with the bubblewrap and cardboard tube using white paint and allow to dry.

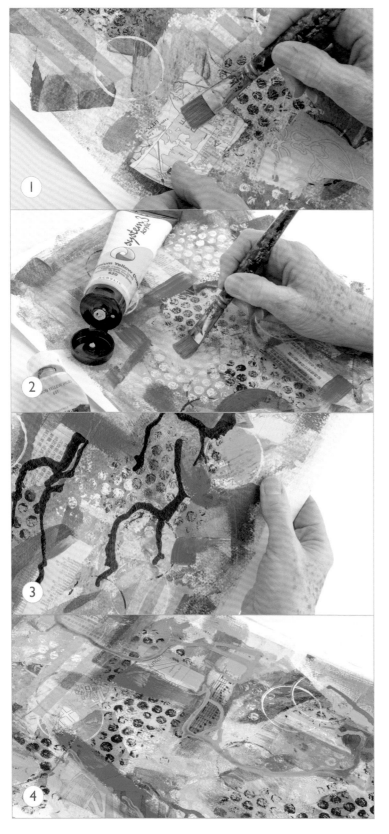

Creating your collage

1. The next step is to add layers of collage. Rip thin papers such as old book pages, paper bags, etc. into narrow strips. Apply a layer of matte medium to the surface of the painting, arrange your collage papers into position and then brush another layer of matte medium over the surface. You can use your brush to flatten down the collage paper or use an old credit card to smooth it out, making sure it's securely stuck down and there are no air bubbles. Small areas of collage work best. If you don't have matte medium you can use a diluted PVA glue instead, although this will leave a shiny surface.

2. Once the collage is dry, add another layer of paint in bright, unsaturated primary colours – red, blue and yellow. I like to vary this and use some of the paint in thick brushstrokes, keeping other areas light and translucent by mixing the paint with either water or matte medium. You can see this in areas where I used yellow paint over the white bubblewrap printing.

3. For your final layer, add some drips in either acrylic ink or watery paint. I like to add black ink for an element of drama. Apply a few drops to the top of the painting and allow it to drip down, holding the paper upright. Move the paper around to allow the drips to flow in different directions. Leave it all to dry.

4. You can vary the effects by experimenting with different paint colours, varying the collage papers or by adding different-coloured inks for the final layer.

Stitching your collage

1. Use your own drawings, look at Pinterest for inspiration or copy my design to draw simple leaf or flower-inspired shapes for your collage. Remember: you are going to have to cut these out and stitch into them, so keep it simple.

2. Draw the design onto the back of your painting – this adds an element of surprise, because until you cut out the design, you won't know which areas of your painting have been selected. Using paper scissors, cut out your shapes and place them on the background sheet, playing around with the arrangement.

3. Take your time with placement and once you're happy with the design, add a tiny amount of glue to the reverse of the collage elements to secure them in place. You are not aiming to glue them down, just to hold them in position.

4. Set up your sewing machine for free motion stitching, feed dogs lowered and embroidery foot on. Use black thread in the bobbin and through the needle. Carefully outline your collage elements using free machine embroidery. Keep to a simple outline but, of course, you can add as much stitching as you wish. Paper is surprisingly robust to stitch into but take care not to stitch over the same areas repeatedly as this will eventually perforate the paper and it may tear.

5. Your stitched collage is now ready to frame and hang on the wall.

< A jug of summer flowers was the inspiration for this collage.

< These greetings cards have been produced by using up small scraps of leftover painting, which have then been stitched.

Taking it further

- Now could be the time to use up all those small scraps of painting that have been cut away, to stitch tiny collages. These can be used to make bespoke greetings cards. The method is exactly the same except that you work small to fit your cards.
- Tiny collages would also make lovely miniature pictures.
- By varying the shapes and using different-colour paints, you can achieve all sorts of effects with your collage. Take a look at some of my examples for ideas.
  Have fun!

USE IT DON'T BIN IT!
Making creative embellishments using recycled materials

∧ Screen-printed and embroidered sampler doodle cloth.

Jessica Grady

Making your own embellishments is something that can be done very easily, much of the time with 'waste' materials that everyone has at home. It's inexpensive and only requires a little imagination and experimentation. The results achieved can be innovative and involve some exciting serendipity! I like the scope of individuality that you can inject into your own embellishments to create something that has combinations of texture, colour and surface quality. Re-using waste, of course, helps to reduce landfill and creates textile projects that are eco-friendly.

This workshop concentrates on creating and making unique embellishments, together with ways of applying these to a prepared background.

∧ Sequin idea using cut, recycled tubing and wire scraps.

Finding your materials – the magic of scrap stores!

As well as saving materials at home, it's well worth looking into your local scrap store to see what treasures they have. Scrap stores collect waste and excess materials from industry that would normally be sent to landfill. Most companies now have to pay to dispose of their perfectly good waste, so instead they donate it to scrap stores which then sort it and re-sell for very low prices to individuals, schools and community groups. I enjoy a good rummage around my local scrap store and have found many interesting and unusual bits and pieces that are impossible to get anywhere else. And don't assume that the stores only stock 'rubbish': for example, if a mill is changing its yarn colour and has left-over wool, this deadstock would normally be thrown out – even though there's nothing wrong with it!

Getting started

Creating sequins

Sequins do not have to be round – they can be any shape, material or size. They can be flat, folded, rolled or pleated into 3D constructions. Making your own sequins rather than using traditional versions will produce a unique finished textile piece, and stimulate creative ideas and innovation in using new materials. I find that using waste and recycled media opens up a whole new world of material possibilities and experimental ideas.

It's a good idea to explore and experiment with waste materials before committing to a large project, as the materials may not behave in exactly the way you want them to, particularly if you are used to working with textiles and other traditional media. I often make loose-leaf collections of materials that I have transformed as a visual idea of how to create my embellishments. Then, if I want to try something out, a piece of material can be easily snipped off and added to a fabric swatch idea.

∨ Experimenting with waste materials.

∨ Square sequins.

Using recycled plastic waste

Try using materials such as:

- old bubblewrap
- cereal packet inners
- plastic lids from butter, soft cheese, etc.
- plastic cartons from vegetables
- plastic wrappers from crisps, biscuits, ground coffee and pasta.

I try to re-use and transform as much plastic waste as possible. By transforming your raw recycled material first – adding colour, melting, cutting and folding – you immediately elevate and create something unusual.

A great technique for transforming recycled plastics along with other waste is to fuse and melt it to create your own sequin sheets.

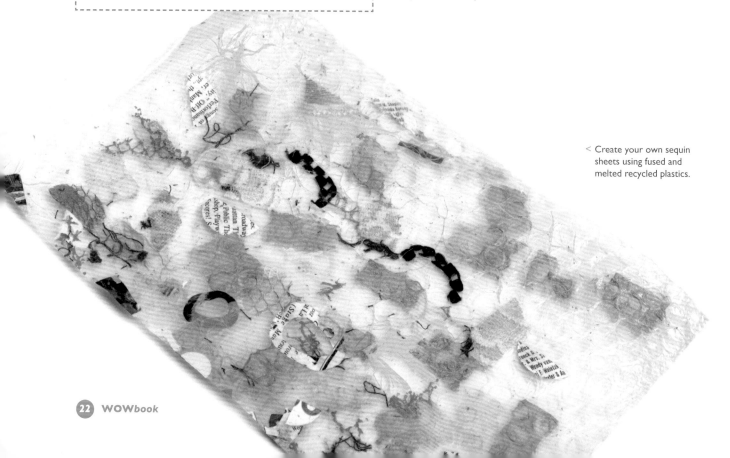

< Create your own sequin sheets using fused and melted recycled plastics.

Making fused sequin sheets

1. Lay your waste plastic on a piece of baking parchment. It may be best to experiment to see how your plastic reacts with heat, as some will shrink and melt away completely (which is not what you want). Recycled bubblewrap and cereal packet inners are good ones to try.

2. Spread your materials across the plastic in your chosen design. Items such as snips of thread-ends, slivers of cut, coloured waste plastic and paper are all great.

   Don't layer-up your materials too thickly as you need to allow the top and bottom layer of plastic to melt together.

3. Top your plastic with a second layer to make a sandwich, cover with parchment and iron on a high setting until the plastic sandwich is smooth and melted on both sides.

4. Wait until completely cool and then unpeel carefully. Should some items require further melting, then just re-iron.

5. Your sequins can now be cut and used as you wish.

> Sample – fused recycled bubblewrap sequins on leatherette.

Making embellishments using recycled metal packaging

Metal has the ability to hold its shape well and you can create some shiny and exciting embellishment ideas with a more constructed and architectural feel. Many household items that we throw away on a regular basis can be washed, kept and transformed into embellished treasure. These include:

- tomato paste tubes – when empty, carefully cut open with scissors and rinse out
- metal foil lids from coffee cartons and dessert pots
- foil wrappers for chocolates and biscuits.

Recycled metal can be cut easily with a paper punch, freehand with scissors or put through a die-cutting machine, to create shapes.

You can dye and paint the recycled foils and metal. Disperse dye, which I use with plastics and other synthetics, works particularly well.

TIP
Different supermarkets use different-coloured metal for their tomato paste!

Turning recycled metal into embellishments and sequins

- You can create origami-like shapes by folding and pinching squares of cut metal sheet/foil into shapes. Poke a hole through the top with a sharp needle and then stitch onto fabric.

- The negative shapes left from paper punches can also be used as 'spangles'.
- Cut your own scales, squares or petals and sew onto fabric as flat sequin embellishments.

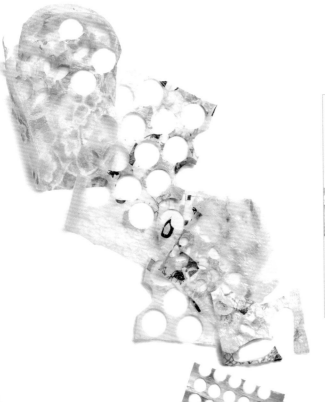

Cutting out your sequins

- Sequins can be hand-cut with scissors. Use a material that doesn't fray, e.g. most recycled foils, metal packaging and plastics.
- Cut out using a die-cutting machine (manual or electric).
- Punch out using a paper punch. These come in a range of sizes and shapes. I use a standard hole punch for making my own very small sequins for some projects.

Patterned painted washers and findings

Washers are one of my favourite embellishments. These can be found in scrap stores, washed-up on the beach and even, sometimes, on the pavement! They come in a range of different materials. The metal variety add a nice weight to fabric and can be transformed easily with a bit of paint. I like to use spray paint as it covers really well and is good for detailing with stencils and resists. You could use acrylic paint or even old nail varnish as alternatives to spruce up your washers.

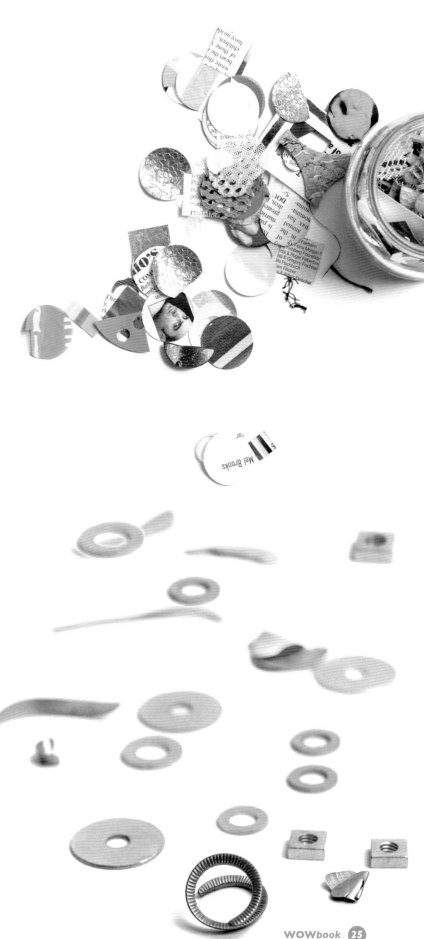

Creating patterned washers

1. To start, make sure your washers are clean and dry. Lay them on some background cardboard or paper – I use old card that I can re-purpose afterwards to avoid waste.

2. Spray the washers all over with a thin coat of spray paint in your chosen colour.

3. If you want a subtle look with the paint colours bleeding together, spray your next layer of paint immediately whilst the first is still wet. For a sharper look, wait until it is touch-dry.

4. Add your stencils or resists. These could be stripes of masking tape, an old lace curtain or a hand-cut paper stencil.

5. When spraying through a stencil, ensure your material is completely flat and spray the paint directly down, not at an angle.

6. Unpeel carefully straight away and repeat with as many colours and patterns as you wish.

7. To achieve a 'splatter' effect, don't press the spray nozzle down fully: the paint will then come out in drips and blobs.

8. To ensure nothing is wasted, your spray-painted backing paper/plastic can be chopped-up or fused together to use as sequins. Thanks to the paint, the painted laces and fabrics can also be cut easily with no fraying!

9. When your washers are dry, they can be used on your fabric samples and stitched into place. Here you can see some alternative patterns and ideas for your painted washers.

Taking it further

Here are some tips and tricks I have discovered during my experiments:

- When experimenting with a new material, I often create several small textile samples and stitch on my embellishments in different ways on each one. This could be a flat repeat pattern on one, and folded layers creating more of a motif pattern on another. Having this library of reference materials helps inform future projects and is a great resource to come back to.
- Use different embroidery stitches to enhance the embellishments. A stitch should not always be just a joining mechanism. Decorative embroidery can both secure the embellishment in place and add extra detail and pattern to a design.
- Think three-dimensionally. As well as stitching flat, can your washer be stitched on its end, or can your cut sequins be rolled and made into a bead?
- Combine materials. Once you have the hang of one type of embellishment, try mixing and layering them together to create multi-textured samples that can spark ideas for larger projects.

∧ Sequin sample with seed stitch detail.

< Large French knots used as a base for embellishments.

The embellishments described in this workshop could be applied to a suitable background, either plain, painted or stitched. They are also a great way of resurrecting a piece that hasn't quite worked, or provide an extra incentive to completing that UFO (unfinished object).

< Folded and flat sequin samples, stitched onto fabric with dyed tubing.

> A layered and stitched sample with dyed nylon washers, sliced and painted foam sequins and punched waste plastic sequins.

> A stitched sample created using spray-painted washers, layered with die-cut recycled paper sequins, painted lace offcuts and recycled metal tubes.

∨ Detail of a mixed technique and media sample.

TULIPMANIA
Turning an image into a mixed media piece

Nikki Parmenter

'Tulipmania' occurred in Holland in the 17th century – a period when the price of tulip bulbs spiralled out of control, with some of the rarest species being purchased at exorbitant prices. Some bulbs cost many times more than an average annual salary. This situation inevitably resulted in a massive economic collapse.

This workshop shows you how to transform a drawing or photograph into a mixed media piece using entrapment and free machine embroidery techniques. Your finished project may be displayed as a two- or three-dimensional object.

MATERIALS AND EQUIPMENT

- Clear PVC plastic (this can be bought by the metre)
- Image to work from
- Ballpoint pen or permanent fine liner
- Cellophane, papers and fabric
- Fairy lights
- Sewing equipment
- Free machine embroidery foot
- Ribbon
- Acrylic paints
- Glue stick

As drawing plays a major role in my work, I wanted to use one of my original sketches of six tulips with leaves.

This technique is very versatile as you can use an original drawing or photograph or an image you have sourced elsewhere (checking copyright first if you use an image from the internet).

Workshop

1. Cut out two pieces of clear PVC and place one on top of your drawing. Trace the outlines of the flowers and leaves onto the PVC using a ballpoint pen or permanent fine liner.

2. For the next step, I drew two butterflies freehand on the other piece of clear PVC. There is no need to draw the whole thing – you can sketch half the butterfly, turn the PVC over and draw the same wing again. If you are not a confident sketcher, you could trace the design.

3. Now for the entrapment technique. This entails making a 'sandwich' of a base layer of clear PVC, a middle layer of patterned plastics, fabrics, iridescent cellophane and gold paper, and the PVC with the traced image on the top.

   In order to place the collaged elements in the correct position in relation to the drawing, place the PVC with the traced image onto a white background and put the clear PVC sheet on the top. You can then position the various pieces of collage more accurately on the top sheet, using the tracing as a guide and leaving a few blank spaces, if you wish. For my piece, I used a mixture of opaque and transparent materials.

I decided I also wanted to create a 'relief' effect, so selected the three central tulips from my drawing and traced the front central petals onto plastic, layering them up in the same way.

4. Secure your pieces using a small amount of glue. Remove the traced image from underneath and place it on top of the collage, using pins to join the three layers together.

5. I used a slightly different process for the butterflies. I placed a single piece of bright blue cellophane between the two sheets of plastic – a clear piece and the drawn image – and added some acrylic paint to the reverse of the drawn image.

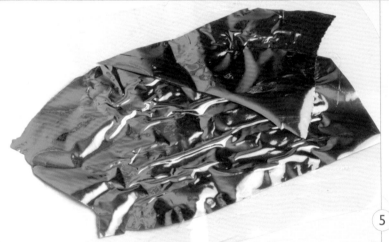

These were then stuck together using a small amount of glue. Place your traced butterfly image on top and pin together.

Adding stitch

1. The next stage is to apply free machine embroidery to the main piece. Use a dark thread. I chose a dark blue thread, and stitched onto the top of the traced lines to create a strong outline.

2. Now use free machine embroidery with a variety of different-coloured threads to embellish the image. You can see here that I used yellow, red, green and orange threads to add texture and detail. I chose to stitch heavily in some areas but to leave some parts less embellished so that the cellophane and fabric show through. For the background, I used a variety of blue threads and stitched around the contours of the tulips to create an organic flowing effect.

   Note that I have not stitched the front petals on the middle three tulips as these are the shapes that are going to be stitched separately and attached later to give a 'relief' effect.

3. Use the same dark thread to stitch around the three separate petal shapes and the butterfly images and once again use a variety of coloured threads to free machine-embroider the details.

4. When the stitching is complete, cut around the shapes very carefully, as close to the edges as possible.

   The separate tulip petal sections and the butterflies should be sewn into the appropriate position by first pinning, then stitching.

   The petals should be attached so that they bend out from the surface, creating a relief effect. The two butterflies are stitched down by just the length of their bodies so that the wings can be folded forward.

The effect can be seen more clearly in this photograph, where the stitched section is used as a three-dimensional piece.

5. Finally, I sewed some loops of ribbon on the reverse which can be used as a hanging mechanism for a panel.

Finishing

There are still some exciting features to add to this piece of work!

- You can create a stained-glass effect if you hang the tulips in a window or against a light source.
- Another suggestion is to take a set of small LED lights and to stitch them onto the reverse of the image. I tried to position the lights against the less densely stitched areas so that they would have maximum impact.
- One final suggestion on how to use this versatile finished piece: I took a two-litre plastic bottle and cut off the top third, thus creating a cylindrical vessel. I then wrapped the sewn panel tightly around the bottle and secured it with some pins. Then … why not switch on the lights and add some pretty fresh flowers? Perfect!

< To create my vessel, I wrapped my sewn panel around an empty plastic bottle, securing it with pins. Add lights and fresh flowers to complete the look.

A FRAGMENT OF SPLENDOUR
Embroidered gold lace on dissolvable fabric

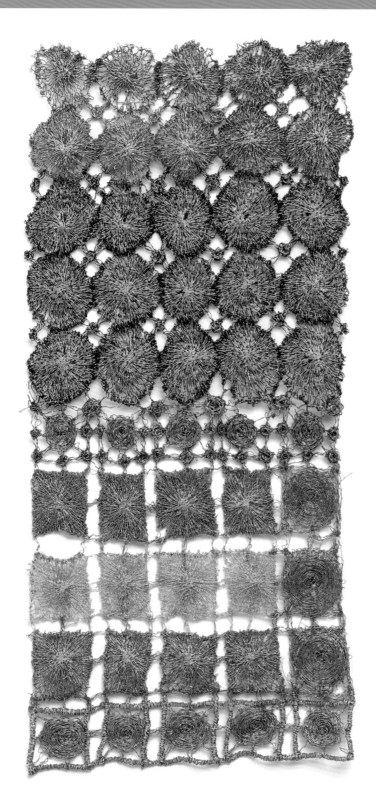

Kate Wells

Working on dissolvable fabric offers some great adventures with embroidery – playing with thread and fabric collage, textural or sculptural forms. It can be a free-form process where anything comes into the mix. However, it's also an exacting medium. Hours of work can simply fall to pieces in the dissolving stage – and it has!

My studio sketchbook is a workplace for samples, thinking on paper, collecting and trialling possibilities. Sometimes, pages have to be removed to make space for additions. I like to attach bookmarks at the edge of a page to indicate a particular theme. In medieval manuscripts and 'books of hours', these are made of vellum and indicate a poem, psalm or special detail.

This project explores the precision of lace-making but with a glorious touch, using metallic thread. The title, 'A Fragment of Splendour', comes from a rich era in the studio when many treasures in my field of interest suddenly came together – medieval goldsmiths' work, jewellery in the Cluny Museum in Paris, early Renaissance gilded paintings and manuscripts, and the 'robes of angels' by Fra Angelico and Botticelli. I wanted to respond to them but with no clear end-product in mind. The idea of making fragments kept it small, with room for study, trial and error. I work on the industrial 'Irish' machine, which extends possibilities to make lovely wide satin stitch up to 12mm, which you can see in the examples here.

∧ Two panels, 8 x 6in (21 x 16cm). Samples of panels exploring a guipure type of lace with solid blocks of leaves joined with wrapped bars to hold all the work together.

> Studio sketchbooks containing samples and ideas.

For this project, we will be using straight stitch on a domestic machine.

You may find this workshop opens up possibilities for your own experiments. The satisfaction of sampling pulls you along with the best question ever: What if …? You could try changing one element such as colour or bobbin-case tension, or a simple change in the direction in stitching, or repetition of a motif.

The main rule is to always cross the stitches over each other, especially at corners. Remember: you are making an entire cloth, so think 'warp and weft' or 'spider's web' so to speak, even though it's a circle being stitched. There must be a foundation of crossing threads to avoid the work having weak spots and gaps.

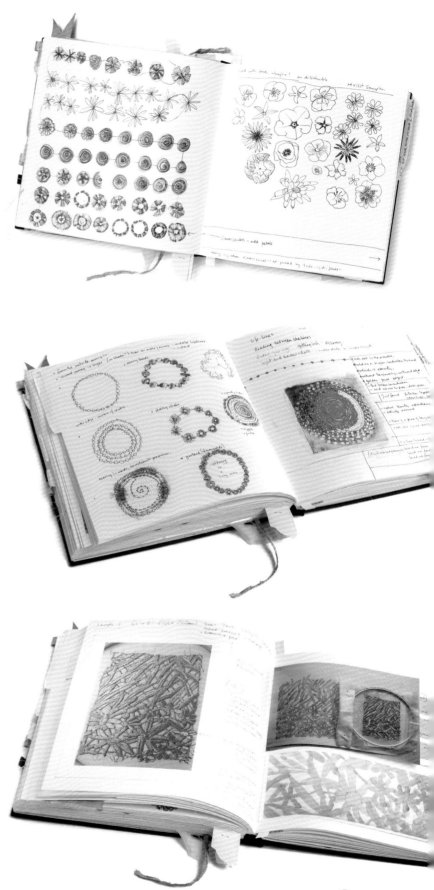

A word about metallic thread. Shredding is inevitable as the metallic foil wrapped around the filament core will rub and break with the friction of the needle. I found that Superior Metallic Thread (I bought mine from Barnyarns) is tightly wrapped and minimises shredding. You may also find that using a 'metallics' needle helps. Test out your needle – too small or too large a hole aggravates this friction.

This is a great project for mindful practice and careful attention which reaps its rewards. It's gentle but very focused.

Good luck! I hope you enjoy the workshop.

Start with a practice sample

It's a good idea to have a practice with the basic shapes before starting on your piece.

1. Stretch a piece of dissolvable fabric in the hoop. The calico-wrapped hoop will grip the fabric. Tighten the hoop-screw and get the fabric really tight, like a drum. This is important. Now draw up your guidelines as shown – wide parallel lines, three circles and three squares and narrow parallel lines – using your fine line pen.

2. Set up your sewing machine with a 'soft' top tension – this minimises shredding and helps the thread to flow lightly through the needle. The bobbin-case should also have a looser tension, so adjust the little screw by degrees until you can see the lower thread pull up to the top of the fabric as you stitch.

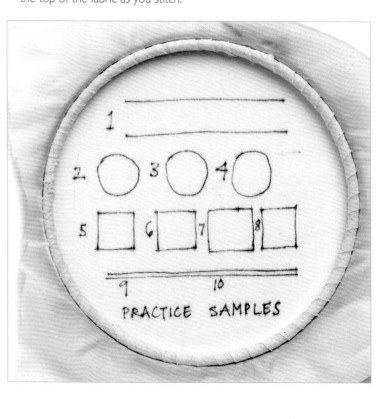

PRACTICE SAMPLES

PRACTICE SAMPLES

These are the basic steps used throughout the project.

3. In your practice hoop:

a   Bring up the bottom thread, lower the presser foot and run lines of stitching accurately between the parallel lines to get your eye in, gradually closing the gap to bring the lines almost side by side. Adjust the bottom tension to get a nice flick of bobbin thread wrapping around the gold. Then move into the circles as follows:

b   Spiral stitch from the centre to the edge.

c   Criss-cross the diameter, gradually rotating around the circle.

d   Combine the two, beginning with the spiral. This creates the 'starburst' motif used in the 'Fragment'.

e   Outline the square, then add a grid of dividing lines (+) followed by a free spiral.

f   Combine the steps in 5 (see the photo above) with criss-crossing lines of stitch, gradually rotating around the square, making sure you catch a stitch over each corner and outline.

g   Outline the square, then run diagonal criss-crossings from edge to edge, corner to corner.

h   Combine 7 with 8 (see above) by adding a densely stitched spiral from the centre outwards.

i   Run several rows of straight stitch between the pen lines.

j   Zigzag, densely wrapping the underneath stitches. This will be used along the bottom of the piece and also create bars between the starburst circles.

Aim to keep the thread intact as you move between shapes – get a flow from shape to shape. This minimises hand-finishing all those loose ends afterwards.

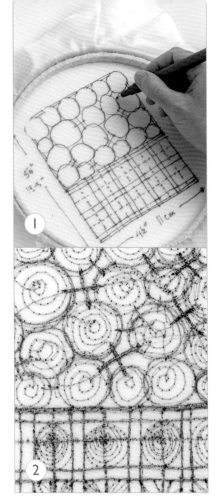

Workshop

1. Stretch-up the hoop tightly with a new piece of dissolvable and draw your design, 5 × 4in (13 × 10cm).

2. The first stage is to stitch all around the design, around each circle and running spirals into each one, flowing from one to another without cutting the thread. In the spaces between some of the circles, make a bar of straight stitches, wrapped with satin stitch. Around the edge, between the circles, make similar bars of straight stitch wrapped with zigzag. Make sure you connect all the lines to circles.

3. Now outline the grid below with two rows of stitching, adding spirals into the top row of squares and star-crossing lines into the bottom row. Even if it looks untidy at this stage, the top layer of stitching will cover the overlaps.

Now you're ready to move onto the real thing.

Mindful stitching

Now for the slow, mindful stitching.

1. With great attention, start to fill the circles with lines of stitching from edge to edge, always going across the centre and occasionally overlapping into the nearby circles. Rotate the hoop to make it an easy forward and backward movement. Keep your nerve as there will be a build-up of threads at the centre and it will feel tough, but the final result is a gorgeous, shimmering star of gold. Get a rhythm and flow as you move from one circle to the next. Relax your posture and feel in balance with the work.

2. Move down to the squares and work the top row in the same way, but crossing from corner to corner, gradually rotating the hoop to fill the square, creating a raised centre as you pass across each time.

   The bottom row of squares is finished with delicious spirals that start in the centre and work out to the edges, wrapping the final circle of stitches over the edge of each square.

3. Along the bottom of the squares, stitch a bar of straight stitches, wrapped with fine satin stitch.

Dissolving the fabric

1. Take the finished stitched fabric out of the hoop, trim away any excess dissolvable fabric from the edges and have a clean pan filled with boiling water ready on the hob.

2. Slip the embroidery into the pan and move the work around in the water as it boils for a minute or so.

3. Turn off the heat and lift out the lace with tongs.

4. Run it under cold water and lay it on a piece of kitchen paper.

   I love it at this stage, all scrunched up and mysterious!

5. Gently stretch the lace out on the block, pressing rather than tugging to get the corners square. Ease the lace into shape, carefully pinning around the edges. Leave it to dry overnight before removing the pins and lifting.

Finishing

There are several ways to present your finished lace, either on a contrast background or a pale one. I chose pale wool Delaine as it shows up the contrasting blue thread against the gold.

> Lace has a life of its own, falling into folds and gathers. This could lead to sculptural forms or it could be combined with other exotic fabrics and materials.

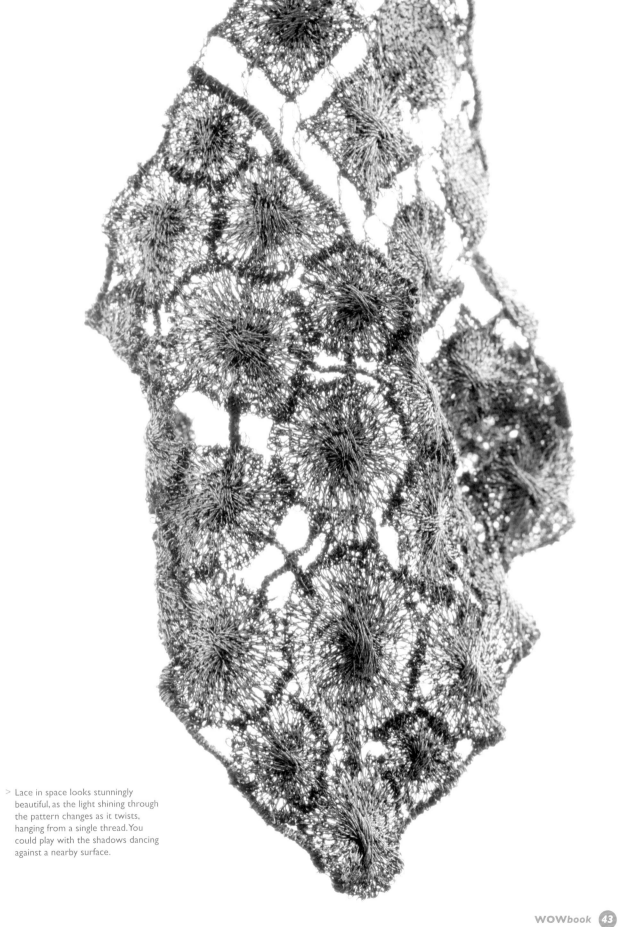

> Lace in space looks stunningly beautiful, as the light shining through the pattern changes as it twists, hanging from a single thread. You could play with the shadows dancing against a nearby surface.

Q Christine, I first came across your work in your gallery at the Festival of Quilts at the National Exhibition Centre in Birmingham UK. I follow you on Facebook and have been a regular visitor to your website for some time now as I just love what you do, how you combine different materials to achieve the finished piece. It always looks so exciting. How did you get started in your creative career?

A I quit smoking! Although that sounds a bit strange, it was quitting smoking that made me look around for something to do whilst watching TV in the evenings. I turned to embroidery – something I already knew how to do from years of being taught by my mum who is a great teacher and avid textile enthusiast – to keep my mind and hands occupied. Drawing, which I had always turned to when bored or looking for distraction, was just not practical with a small child in the house, as the safe space and concentration required was constantly being broken. Knitting was relatively expensive and not something I felt could be justified with a family to care for. So I rifled through my mum's stuff and found some transfers in an old magazine, along with cheap stranded threads, and promptly sewed a couple of cushion covers.

∨ *The Old Sea Wall.* 1992. City & Guilds Part 2 embroidered panel. This piece had a screen-printed base image on vinyl, with tissue paper, papier-mâché, paper pulp and cling film used to add texture, with machine embroidery.

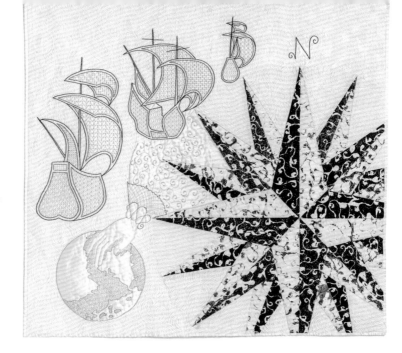

I quickly realised that sewing gave me something more than just a distraction; it gave me satisfaction. I wanted more – I wanted to be able to make my own things and not to have to use a pattern developed by someone else. I took City & Guilds (C&G) in both Embroidery and in Patchwork & Quilting, and then went on to do the Part 2 (now Diploma) level in Embroidery in order to learn about metal thread work.

I began teaching alongside mum, covering the design element of the C&G course. As a qualified teacher, this seemed a natural step for me, and my career just took off from there. I took over the whole C&G teaching when mum retired, adding in other evening textile courses and creating my own work in my spare time.

I found I needed to make resolved pieces to continue to give me that sense of satisfaction that had drawn me into working with textiles, as well as creating samples for my classes. I would take risks which generally meant that I then had plenty of problems to solve along the way to making a final piece – adding another layer to that feeling of fulfilment!

It was a final life-changing experience that pushed me firmly into taking myself seriously as an artist. At 17, my stepson suffered a life-altering road traffic accident and, after a year of constant support, he went into a rehab centre which allowed me time to take a step back and re-evaluate my life. At that stage, I realised that there was no point in waiting for there to be a better time to push for achievement, as something catastrophic could happen and get in the way; it was safer to make my own 'luck' and do it immediately. This made me take a more professional approach to working, to making, to teaching and to learning.

At that point I came across Claire Benn and Leslie Morgan at Committed to Cloth and have worked with, and alongside them, ever since. They have been an inspiration to me, as well as being role models for that professionalism I was seeking.

Q I consider myself a mixed media textile artist because of the variety of fabrics, materials and mediums I like to use in my work. How would you describe your textile art?

A For many years I made quilts because I put two or three layers together and stitched them together in some way. Or so I thought.

When I look back at what I made, in light of how I now describe my work as 'mixed media textiles', I realise I was always doing this. This is possibly the result of the mix of Embroidery and Patchwork C&G courses, which encouraged me to work with paper, plastic and a whole variety of materials above and beyond the normal fabric variety. They gave me a *lot* of processes to call upon, admittedly all at a very basic skill level, but enough to be able to call upon and develop in order to use appropriately in a piece of work.

In 2003, I made *The Age of Exploration* which involved a gesso lamination process. I used this to create weathered-looking white and black silk patterned fabrics for use in a mariner's compass section of the work. In 2004, I created *Faint Hope* which involves muslin hexagons wrapped around clear acrylic 'papers' along with printed paper sandwiches shaped as hexagons, with netting running in the middle of the sandwich. These were definitely quilts in the true definition of the word, but involved using a mix of media.

∧ *The Age of Exploration.* 2003. Hever Castle Region 2 Challenge Winner. The mariner's compass section was produced using fabric made by gesso lamination which was then foundation pieced. The rest was machine quilted on silk, with hand embroidery.

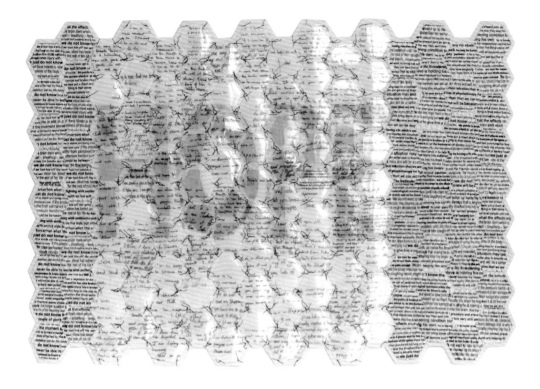

< *Faint Hope*. 2004. This piece was exhibited at Danson House in Tracy Chevalier's exhibition 'The Things We Do in Bed' in 2014. The central section is pieced using English paper piecing (EPP) over acrylic 'papers' using muslin. The outer sections were laminated paper and netting. The word HOPE is painted on the reverse of the piece, though it is only very faint.

∨ *Fading ii*. This is the latest piece in my dementia series, shortlisted for a Fine Art Textiles Award at the Festival of Quilts in 2019. Pieced using laminated, painted and printed transparent fabrics with EPP, hand-sewn together and hung showing both sides.

This is how I now define my work: mixed media textiles. I continue to call upon some of the traditional processes I learned in my C&G courses, but try to push them forward through the use of different fabrics and contexts. I worked more with English paper piecing (EPP) for my work *Fading ii* in 2019, but used transparent fabrics that had been printed, painted and laminated with a repeating phrase.

I developed a type of foundation appliqué for the transparent paper lamination hanging made in collaboration with Sarah Welsby for our unFOLD exhibition 'Button Box' in 2018.

∨ *Fading ii*. Detail showing a selection of textures and tones created by different mark-making techniques on transparent fabrics.

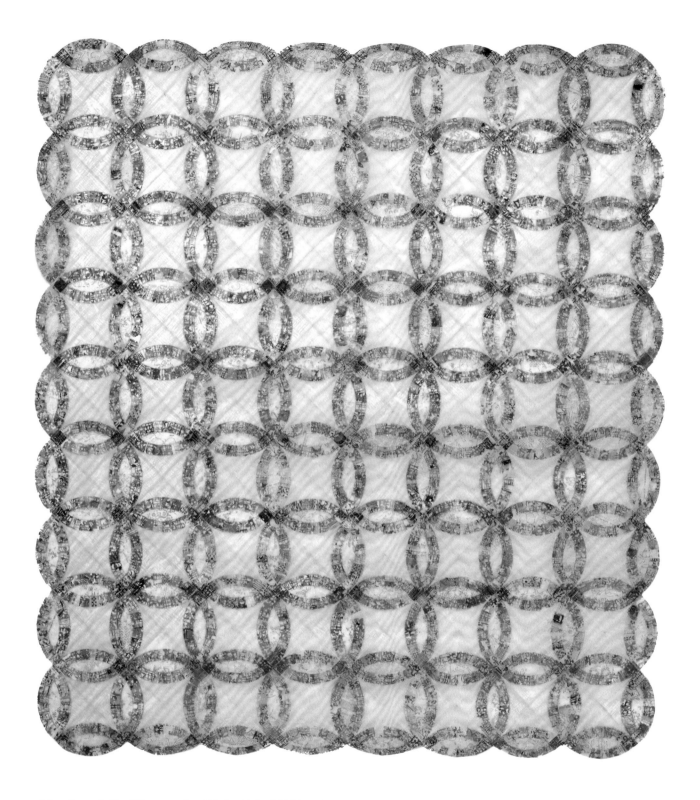

∧ *Love, Honour & Obey.* This was produced jointly with Sarah Welsby and exhibited in the unFOLD gallery at the Festival of Quilts in 2018. The double wedding ring blocks were made using paper lamination fabrics which were then applied on papers to achieve an accurate block.

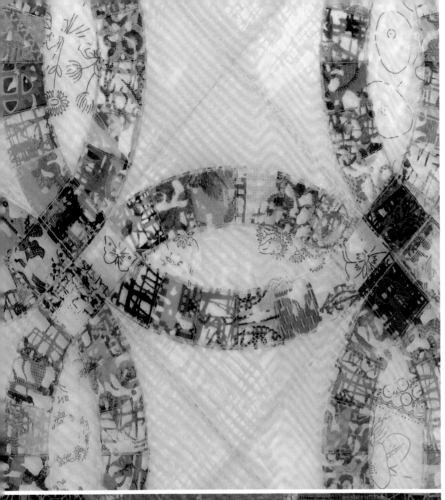

< *Love Honour & Obey*. Detail showing the papers used for lamination, including photo images from an annual of *The Embroideress Magazine* from 1922, and blue embroidery transfers taken from magazines from the 1950s and 1960s.

Q Everyone has their favourite technique and preferred medium. I'm always drawn to anything that can produce a rusty or distressed surface, but which medium/ technique do you prefer?

A Paper lamination is one of my favourite techniques. This came about originally as I wanted photographs of my father to use in a series on dementia, which has yet to be completed as I have so much material about this condition, and I am constantly learning when talking with people.

Paper lamination is great for two reasons: I can work with paper – copies of photographs or marks that have been made on paper don't always translate to fabric. I can also work with ideas about transparency, fragmentation, layers, blurring – all ideas that work well for dementia but also work for other themes involving absence that I have since moved onto.

Essentially I don't stick with one process. I like to start from scratch with plain fabric and have control over all the marks on that fabric, be they dyed, printed or stitched. This is because I work with ideas first. The pieces that I make and all the processes that go into those pieces have to fit with the aim or the rationale of the idea. That suggests that I plan my work, which I do, but often with fabric that has already been created rather than starting completely from scratch. When I am in the mood or place to make fabric, my consistent work with a theme allows me to make on spec and experiment with that idea in mind, so when I need fabric, there is a palette to choose from to suit the mood.

< *Fragmented Networks*. 2010. This was my first major piece in the dementia series, made by collaging paper lamination photo images, with gesso lamination adding texture in the bottom right corner. The whole piece was then machine quilted.

> *Standing on the Shoulders of Giants*. 2019. This was produced for the Quilt Art exhibition at Menier Gallery, London. It is a copy of an old quilt I had in my possession, created from paper lamination fabrics which were then machine stitched onto foundation paper.

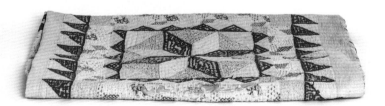

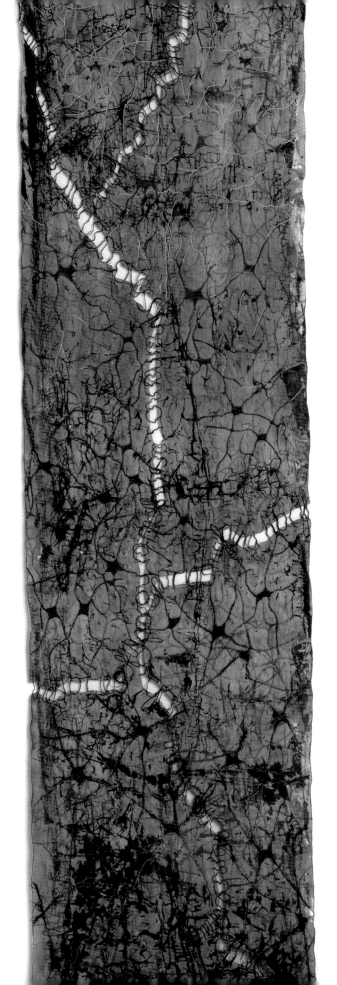

< *Slipping Between the Cracks*. 2018. This was made for a Quilt Art exhibition at the International Quilt Study Center, Nebraska USA. The cloth was produced by printing, mark-making and flour paste resist, and machine quilted using a very loose tension towards the bottom of the piece to represent bleeding. The whole piece was then split and put back together again using machine embroidered words to join the separate pieces.

I also love to stitch, whether that is by hand or machine. I decide which based on a couple of factors: what will be appropriate for the idea, and what would be better functionally for this fabric/process. I then decide which project to work on, as I may have several on the go at once, depending on how much daylight time I have. I will often choose to work on a project that I know will be best made by hand if I will only be able to work in the evenings, when I can stitch sitting in front of the TV. If I have a lot of daylight time to stitch, then I can consider working on a piece that requires machine work.

∨ A palette of fabrics from my stash.

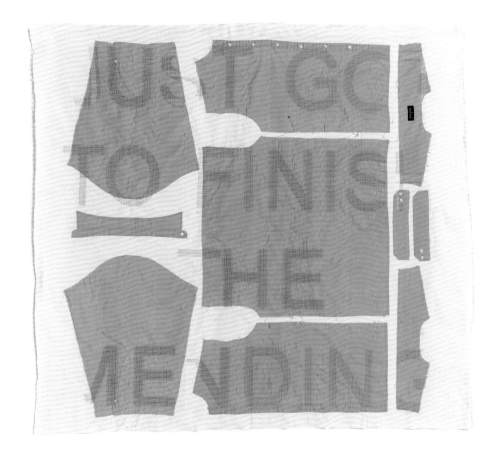

> *I'll Be Up In A Minute.* 2018. This piece was made for unFOLD's 'Button Box' gallery at the Festival of Quilts. The caption says: 'Just got to finish the mending'. An old shirt was deconstructed and tacked onto a backing with the words being created using hand embroidered darning stitch.

Q I find my best work is done early morning (that's the time I get the most peace, too!). When is your most creative time?

A Being self-employed and having to rely on my income to make ends meet, I generally have to work at all times of the day. Part of my professionalism is to try to work at something even if I don't feel like it. That is increasingly hard to do with the admin for the studio and screens to make for the Thermofax business.

I have tried to divide up the day so that I could work in the morning when the light was good and my brain was clear but, unfortunately, that is also a good time for writing articles and generating publicity material. I have given up trying to work like that and just get on with whatever job is prioritised for that day until it is completed. Sometimes, that results in stitch work being put on the back burner for several days in a row.

I spent several years when I was working nearly full-time at college in a managerial role, doing my stitching at home in the evenings. I was lucky at this time to be making the basic fabrics at Committed to Cloth on a Saturday with a bunch of fabulous people who are still close friends – students and teachers. I got to create some things in daylight, but the stitching was all done at night and on Sundays!

This means that you don't get the luxury of working at your best time of the day but the nature of textile work is that there are processes and jobs that have to be done, are repetitive and don't require a lot of creative input. The other bits that do require more creativity can be done at a time when this may be more successful, or at least have more daylight.

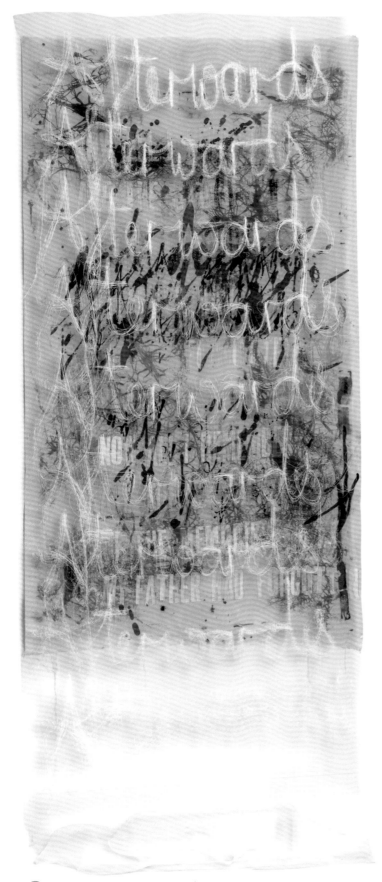

< *Afterwards iii.* This was made for my solo gallery at the Festival of Quilts in 2015. Drop cloth from previous print sessions was used as the background, with a machine embroidered transparent cloth hung in front with the words 'Afterwards' repeated. This word becomes more and more out of control as we head towards the bottom of the piece.

Q This is a question that most artists have to deal with at some time or another: Do you ever get creative block and, if so, how do you deal with it?

A I am lucky in that I work with creative people at my studio, but unlucky in that I only have time to make very few large pieces each year. I am also a member of a textile group who are constantly finding ways of encouraging each other's creativity by swapping work, sketchbooks and/or objects that we all have to take inspiration from to generate small works. I rarely have time for a block!

However, I did experience a major block after my Masters degree. I had spent all of 2015 making work for a solo gallery at the Festival of Quilts, making a hanging for another gallery in that Festival, and also creating work for my MA. By the time I had completed all the work and paperwork for the degree show, I was finished. I sat around and moped. I thought I was never going to make a piece of work again, or certainly nothing that would be as good as the work I had made that year.

I knew I had to get out of this to be any use to my students if nothing else. So I enrolled on a drawing course: something different, something to make me do something each week. And perhaps key: something with no expectations. I never completed it (it was a 10 week course) as by week 6 I had an idea which I needed to work on, and I was off again.

Q Your studio is a fabulous building and the classes and workshops you teach always look very interesting and inspiring. Can you tell us a bit more about how your studio came about and the workshops you offer?

A In 2012, I was offered the opportunity to take voluntary redundancy from my position at college, and by then I realised that I probably had enough knowledge that I could run my own studio along the lines of Committed to Cloth. Leslie and Claire were super-supportive and a lovely venue was found in the centre of town by the railway station.

From there, I was able to start regular once-a-month classes which also gave me the time and opportunity to continue making work. I am lucky enough to have a niece, Amy, who is a branding expert and she gave me many pointers as to how to market the studio, now known as Studio 11.

With Amy's help the studio grew and, in 2014, I started offering intensive textile courses with teachers other than myself. Eastbourne is a fabulous holiday town with lots of accommodation and restaurants for all budgets, and this was an obvious step forward for the studio. I was able to arrange for a wide range of excellent tutors to come down to the south coast, with the extra benefit of being able to use the coastal environment as inspiration for many of the retreats on offer.

I enjoy teaching skills-based classes so am able to use the facilities and space to teach dyeing and printing processes from scratch. I feel that my real strength lies in being able to help and facilitate people to develop their own work, complete projects, solve problems and move work forward. Many of the monthly classes offered are creative development classes for people with all sorts of textile interests. I've worked with weavers, knitters, embroiderers and quilters, giving the studio groups a diverse vibe, and students enjoy the wide range of work being done in classes.

In 2019, I wasn't able to meet the landlord's expectation of a vastly increased rent for the space I was currently working in, and the studio moved to smaller premises, even closer to the sea. Studio 11 is now housed in an old chapel, full of character and light, and we were all just settling into a new routine of classes when the Covid-19 pandemic hit.

Like Committed to Cloth, I've been trying to build a community of people who love working with textiles. When lockdown came along, I was keen to help everyone get through a difficult and unknown situation. I took the classes online and the experience of making videos and running Zoom tutorials encouraged me to take some of my other 'travelling' workshops online. I'm now enjoying another aspect of teaching, seeing work develop over a longer period than a 'normal' 3–5 day workshop allows. This also enables me to meet students from all over the world.

∨ *Afterwards iii*. Detail.

Q What do you enjoy most about teaching? For me, I find that being able to pass on my knowledge and skills in mixed media textiles is very satisfying and rewarding, especially when you see students running with the ideas you have given them.

A I enjoy seeing the excitement that comes from learning a new skill. Students are endlessly creative and experimental and, when they realise that there is potential in the skills being learned that might take them further than a short workshop actually allows, this gives me a real buzz. I like to nurture this creativity and confidence via long-term contact with students in the studio, doing once-a-month classes rather than short-term intense workshops.

I'm grateful that I learned my skills as a teacher over many years at college and spent several years observing other teachers and helping them develop their skills. I am passionate about providing good-quality facilities and teaching people who are passionate about their own work. They deserve that.

∨ 2020 work in progress. *Temari* (traditional Japanese embroidered thread balls) made in the traditional way but with handmade paper, thread and wire allowed to rust around the outside.

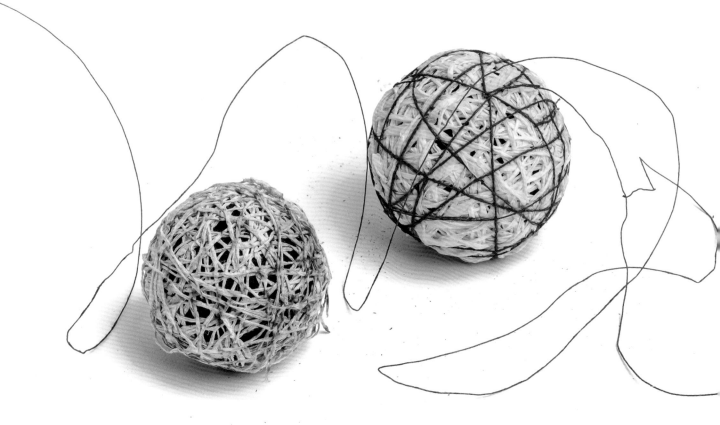

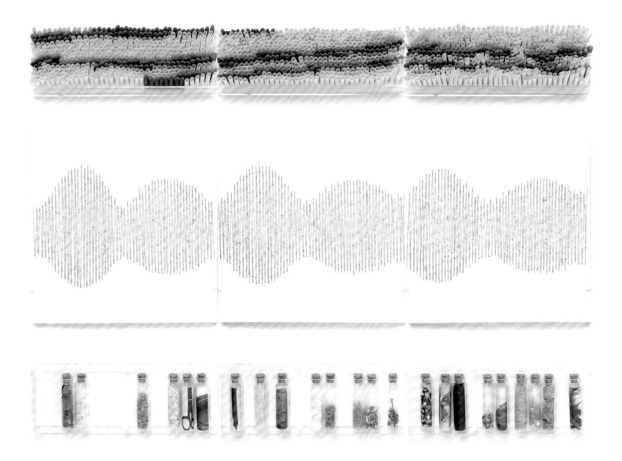

Q For most of us, the recent pandemic and the social distancing guidelines have put all our well-laid plans on hold, with workshops, talks and exhibitions being cancelled for the time being. What is on the horizon for you creatively and how have your teaching and workshops been affected?

A My last solo exhibition was in 2015 and I now feel that I have developed the work around dementia sufficiently to work towards building another solo show. I would like to take this into a more open art environment rather than just showing to textile enthusiasts. It's a hard road to tread, as textiles are much misunderstood within the wider art world, despite all the rhetoric around craft being more acceptable. I've stepped back from being a member of Quilt Art in the hope that this will give me more time and opportunity to develop ideas that are a little more installation-based.

In creating the online workshops, I have the opportunity to develop ideas for these that the short workshops don't allow. So I'm working with more creative ideas and having to demonstrate them whilst filming, which should result in some more fabrics to work with – always exciting and inspiring.

I am also looking back at some of my skills learned and developed many years ago which I thought I had left behind, such as the Japanese craft of *temari* (traditional embroidered thread balls). These embroidered balls had a particular place in my work when I was taking my City & Guilds and then teaching short day workshops, but I stopped making them in the 1990s as they did not, at the time, offer me any room for contemporary development. However, my perception of the 'traditional' has moved on and I am now looking forward to using this skill again with new materials and a different concept behind them.

∧ *Coastal Diary*, section April to June. Part of a full year of Waves, Tides and Findings, made for Curious as an Object Gallery with unFOLD at the Knitting & Stitching Show 2016. Waves constructed from paper straws, tidal range stitched, and findings cut up into glass specimen bottles.

SAME SEA, DIFFERENT BOAT

ISOLATION STORIES IN LOCKDOWN

with *Sue Brown*, *Louise Asher* and *Liske Johnson*

Sue is an artist/printmaker, and Louise and Liske are textile artists. All have businesses providing creative workshops in printmaking, stitch and textiles in Cheltenham, Nottingham and Bromsgrove UK respectively. Like many others, they suddenly found themselves without work and income due to the coronavirus lockdown.

By mid-May of lockdown, creativity became difficult for many folk. The people whom these talented tutors usually inspired were finding the situation difficult. It was not the creative opportunity they imagined, with more time at home giving an opportunity to finish projects or start new ones. Sue, Louise and Liske wanted to encourage creativity and, with this in mind, started a small project, asking people to create a 4 x 4in (10 x 10cm) collagraph plate. Collagraph printmaking is a process in which a textured plate, which can be simply made from card and glue, is inked up and put through a press. The variation in textures produces a range of different print tones.

These 'plates' were posted to Sue who printed them out using her etching press before posting them back to the contributor to add stitch. The intention was to combine the stitched prints to create a quilt describing our emotional and physical experiences in lockdown. *Same Sea, Different Boat* acknowledges that we all experienced lockdown, but not all in the same way.

∧ *Same Sea, Different Boat* quilt ... with spaces for more contributions.

Initially, Sue, Louise and Liske thought they might have around 30 squares to print – with perhaps another 20 stitched pieces to make a quilted panel. They were astonished to receive over 200 collagraph plates from all over the world. To date, they have received over 300 squares with which they have created five quilted panels, with more squares still arriving.

isolation story 2020. LOCK DOWN:

Sue, Louise and Liske explain how this project came about …

Sue: When lockdown was announced, I halted all face-to-face classes and set up a WhatsApp group to stay in contact with my students and colleagues. It was all so sudden and shocking initially. Having to finish the term early made me feel guilty, so I set up a weekly creative prompt on my blogspot, with small projects that I could build up each week. I also kept up a presence on social media. For me it was all about keeping in touch.

Louise: I agree, the start of lockdown felt somewhat surreal without any clear idea of how long it would go on, nor of the long-term effects of the pandemic. I decided that the most important thing was to be open and stay in touch with artists and participants. It goes without saying that safety was a priority and I also kept a strong presence on social media. The support network of the creative world was amazing, so I never felt on my own. I received many messages from students and friends who weren't able to concentrate and find inspiration whilst in isolation, so I set up a weekly Zoom meeting (I had never heard of Zoom before). For an hour a week, we could share ideas, stitch or draw without pressure or judgement. It was around this time that Sue contacted me about an idea for a small (little did we know) project. It was the perfect opportunity to come together as a community and share our experiences through print and stitch.

Liske: It's true – it was the strangest time. I think I've been through every emotion at one point or other! Mild panic was the first one, but then I came to quite enjoy the quiet life that followed. I think, like most of us, I didn't expect the lockdown to last as long as it did, so it was impossible to plan. I have two young boys (aged eight and five) so my focus was very much on them, and work had to take a back seat. They were a good distraction. Like both of you, I wanted to keep everyone creative. Initially, my partner, Claire, and I started to offer daily creative prompts – just simple design exercises that anyone could do. Needless to say, as time went on we started to run low on ideas but continued to share everything we were doing and any new ideas in order to keep our ladies (and the odd gent!) feeling inspired.

^ Collagraph plates made of card and wood glue.

Sue: It was around mid-May that I noticed creativity flagging. I know I was finding inspiration difficult. Cleaning behind my fridge one day (yes, I was that desperate!) I thought – this is not good, I need to do something about this.

At the start of lockdown, I had encouraged my printmaking group to make a collagraph square and send it to me. Using my press, I printed them all together as one large patchwork on paper. This led me to think that it would make a good quilt. I thought that if everyone sent me a collagraph plate, I could print it on fabric and ask them to add a bit of stitch. My mailing list is mainly printmakers so I thought Louise and Liske's groups might enjoy a printmaking challenge – and my groups may like a stitching challenge.

Before I changed my mind, I picked up the phone and floated the idea to both Louise and Liske. Looking back, what did you think about that conversation?

Liske: I was totally flattered to be asked! My 'following' is not in the same league as yours, or that of Hope & Elvis [the name of Louise's studio]. I also thought what a great way to engage our communities! You'll remember that I was a little apprehensive about how much time I'd be able to commit, but that hasn't been an issue at all. I love the title *Same Sea, Different Boat* and feel it captures the moment, and the project, perfectly. I've said so many times to family and friends that everyone's situation in the pandemic is different, and you just have to do what's right for you.

Louise: I loved the idea straight away and, like Liske, thought it was a great way to connect with everyone. The name fits it perfectly – we are all dealing with the same global pandemic differently.

Sue: A 4in (10cm) square is not a daunting size and I've been amazed at how much people have packed onto them. For my own contribution, I decided to stick with an earlier idea I had about a 'Covid Corvid'. For those of you who know my work, crows are a theme, but as a printmaker, I felt an edition would be appropriate. There are 19 Covid Corvids throughout the quilt. How about you two – what were your inspirations?

^ *Covid Corvid* runs through the quilt as an editioned collagraph. The numbers are stitched.

Louise: Being such a people person, I really struggled with the feeling of being trapped and alone. That sounds kind of strange with three girls, a husband, two dogs and two hamsters – our house is never quiet! My square features a caged lion trapped from the outside world, with a little neon thrown in.

Liske: I made a collagraph square that was inspired by one of our many family walks. We were at the top of the Lickey Hills, Birmingham, and suddenly a rainbow appeared. Lucas, my youngest son, said 'Mummy, do you think the sky made a rainbow to say thank you to all of the nurses?' Just thinking about it now brings a lump to my throat – it was a very heart-warming moment. I also created a collaged piece. The background was fabric printed by my mum. It was important to me that she was on the quilt somehow, and on it I appliquéd a sunflower seedling. At the start of lockdown, the boys and I really enjoyed planting seeds and watching them grow, week by week.

< Liske's rainbow square (left) together with her sunflower seedling (above).

> Louise's square features a caged lion, trapped from the outside world.

Sue: My mailing list and Instagram followers were keen to make a collagraph square but I also loved the letters that came with the work, expressing concern about how their first ever plate would print, and was amazed at how many I received to ink-up. So many people had a go at the print element.

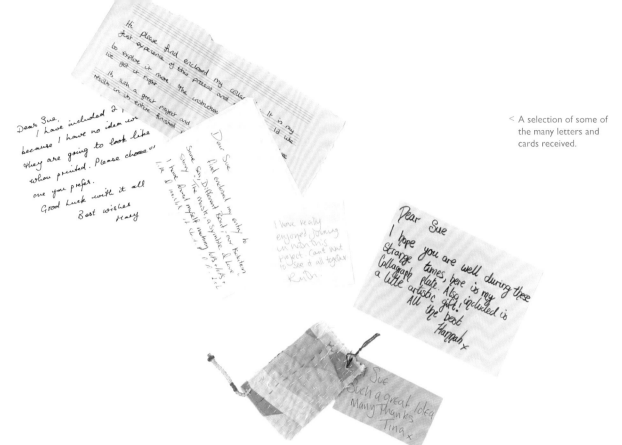

< A selection of some of
the many letters and
cards received.

Liske: Yes, initially I was a little worried that many of my 'regulars' wouldn't have used this technique before, and I thought it might put them off. In fact, I think it had the opposite effect and everyone relished the challenge of trying something new.

Louise: I knew instantly that this project would catch the imagination of fellow creatives but never in my wildest dreams was I prepared for it to grow into something truly incredible. The squares hold so many emotions – fear, hope, sadness and joy. The time, love and energy that have been put into each and every one is breathtaking.

Sue: I would just like to announce here that I have never made a quilt before. Had it not been for the constant guidance of Catherine Kingzett, a textile artist in her own right and my personal quilting guide, together with fellow artist Caroline McCatty for her constant support and help with tacking, this project would not look quite the same. I got you two on board for your textile experience: was I right?

> Our *Same Sea, Different Boat* quilt now consists of five separate panels of collagraphed and hand-stitched squares from all over the world. The quilt is being exhibited at the Museum in the Park, Stroud, Gloucestershire until 20 December 2020, moving to Salisbury Arts Centre, Wiltshire for January 2021 and then onto the Harley Gallery in Nottingham UK, March to June 2021.

Louise: Being honest, my quilting knowledge is also zero! Each and every square deserves the utmost respect so it was such a relief to have guidance from an experienced quilter. Having Sue and Liske at the other end of the phone has also been a bit of a life-saver for sharing our ups and downs.

Liske: Ha! A quilter I am not. I think because my mum was known for patchwork and quilting, people expect me to know what I'm doing. My degree was in printed textiles – there was literally no sewing involved. Over the years, I've taken part in the odd workshop and I was grateful that the quilting for this project was nice and simple. We all owe a big 'thank you' to Catherine for her guidance along the way. I felt comforted by the fact that none of us are 'quilters' – we were learning together.

Sue: Now the quilt is complete … but is it? Everyone has experienced the effects of lockdown, the restrictions and, in some cases, the change in lifestyle, and this will continue for quite some time. We intend to make the quilt open-ended, allowing us to add more squares as they arrive beyond the deadline. Also, we want to exhibit it and encourage further additions to the piece as it tours around the country, asking visitors to print and stitch a contribution.

Louise: The *Same Sea, Different Boat* quilt will be such an important document of the global pandemic through the medium of print and stitch. I would love to exhibit the quilt all over the world, for it to be admired and added to. It's such an amazing story for future generations.

Liske: It really is a piece of textile history. I really hope we will be able to exhibit at the big quilt shows, such as the Festival of Quilts. I have every confidence that it will end up being a well-travelled quilt! Well done, Sue, for seeing the potential to document this period of time in textile form.

The quilt is a metaphor for how the effects of the quarantine have isolated us, yet we have all been part of it. Making the piece open-ended also illustrates that Covid-19 will continue to shape our lives.

Everyone has their isolation story and people can still become part of the bigger picture.

Same Sea, Different Boat: 2020.

Sue: I run workshops in printmaking and mixed media from the yard:ARTspace in Cheltenham UK. I'm keen to demystify collagraphs – a flexible process using easily found materials: card, textured wallpaper and wood glue. I have recently been experimenting with printing onto fabric substrates.

www.theyardartspace.com
www.suebrownprintmaker.
blogspot.com

Louise: I am the owner of Hope & Elvis, a studio situated on the Welbeck Estate, Nottinghamshire UK. I curate a programme of workshops with invited artists and makers. It's a studio full of warmth, materials, creativity and great food. I have a huge passion for fibre art and screen printing.

www.hopeandelvis.com

Liske: I run a variety of textile workshops, short courses and regular art textile groups at Littleheath Barn Studio, Bromsgrove UK, with my closest friend Claire Lundy. Littleheath Barn Studio was the resident studio for my mum, textile artist Ineke Berlyn, who sadly passed away in 2017. I run the studio as a happy place for local creatives.

www.littleheathbarnstudio.com

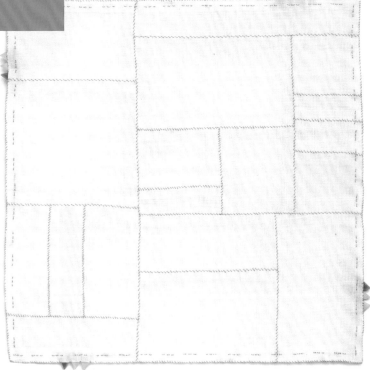

^ *Spring Green #2*. Thrift was valued in Confucian philosophy so I have used the small leftover pieces of fabric from the main piece to make a second smaller piece of work. Pieced with *garumsol* seams (whip stitch).

Sara Cook

With a professional seamstress for a mother and an uncle who was a Savile Row tailor, I was never far from fabric and sewing advice as I grew up.

As an adult, I honed my creative skills training as a theatrical costume maker in Liverpool and later at Glyndebourne Opera House. I enjoyed the most demanding and rewarding job in theatrical costuming and there developed a love of teaching.

I established the Brighton Fashion and Textile School in 2012 to teach accredited courses and offer City & Guilds qualifications in Patchwork and Quilting. Completing the qualification as a judge for The Quilters' Guild of the British Isles meant I was once again a student and could continue to learn even more about the wonderful world of stitching.

When I first encountered Chunghie Lee's work at the Festival of Quilts in 2009, I was struck by the unfamiliarity of the fabrics and the seams. Her work was inspired by all those unknown Korean women who had made beautiful wrapping cloths collectively known as *bojagi*. This led me to start researching Korean wrapping cloths and to incorporate the techniques into my own working practice.

Attending the Korean Bojagi Forum in Seoul in Korea in 2016 was the culmination of my research and gave me the opportunity to meet Chunghie Lee and many other international textile artists. As a guest exhibitor and lecturer at the 2018 Korean Bojagi Forum, I exhibited my work to a Korean audience for the first time. In my gallery exhibition 'Transparency and Transition' at the Festival of Quilts in 2019, I invited a number of international textile artists similarly inspired by *bojagi* to show their work in the UK and to share with a wider audience the wonderful possibilities of this Korean textile tradition.

A travel bursary awarded to me by The Quilters' Guild of the British Isles, recognising my expertise in this area of textiles, allowed me to carry out further research with *bojagi* expert Youngmin Lee in California USA.

For me, working within the boundary of *bojagi*, exploring translucent fabrics such as ramie and silk organza, combined with the narrow seaming techniques, allows me to explore light passing through overlapping colours. The seaming structure creates a further linear dimension often revealed in the shadows that they cast. The design and symbolism in *bojagi* continually inspires me to reflect on how I work. One way this has influenced me is to find ways of using up every leftover scrap of fabric from each piece of work I create. Even the trimmings from the seams and the ends of threads are made into more fabric.

∧ *Spring Green #2*. Detail. *Setlam sangchim*, three decorative stitches and three *JakSsi* decorative pine nuts embellish the edge and symbolise wishes for good luck and happiness.

> *Spring Green #3*. Made from all the tiny pieces left from trimming the seams from the main piece. I like to use everything up so that nothing is wasted. The fabric is precious. Decorated with *bakgi mae dup*, bat knots in silk organza that symbolise wishes for good fortune.

Currently I'm working on *Green Light*, a piece celebrating the coming of spring. The hopeful sight of green buds and the blush of white blossom on blackthorn bushes inspired me to capture the feeling of renewal that this season brings. I am working with a new fabric, a silk and ramie mix, and exploring a new seam, *Sam Sol*.

My book *Bojagi: Design and Techniques in Korean Textile Art* is the culmination of ten years of research into this ancient tradition.

www.bojagiuk.com

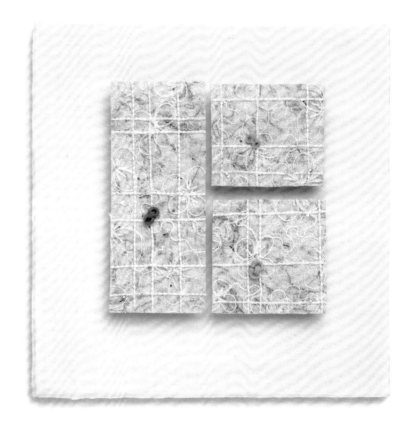

Gina Ferrari

For as long as I can remember, I've had a desire to create. My childhood memories are filled with producing endless drawings, handmade books or comics, miniature fairy gardens, hand-stitched dolls' clothes and numerous other handmade items that were often foisted onto my family as gifts. I was definitely one of the original Blue Peter generation, never passing by an opportunity to convert a plastic squeezy bottle or cardboard loo-roll tube into a work of art!

Moving into my teenage years, my days were filled with more drawing and fashion illustrations, whilst I dreamt of going to art college and having a career in illustration or fashion design. As often happens, my life didn't follow that particular path and despite taking A level art, I eventually found myself teaching

∧ *Lacuna.* This lace book came about through ideas of concealment and revelation. It was built-up from hundreds of small pieces of lace that had been given to me by readers of my blog. Each fragment came with a story – such as having been part of a wedding gown – and the stories were stitched into the lace pages.

secondary school maths – a far cry from that fantasy career. Marriage and motherhood followed and as a stay-at-home mum to four boys, my days were filled with all sorts of creativity that often involved elaborate birthday cakes and fancy dress costumes.

It was during this time that – by chance – I ended up taking a Level 1 City & Guilds (C&G) course in machine embroidery. I was totally hooked by this previously untapped potential of my sewing machine. Who knew such things were possible? I certainly shan't be making curtains again any time soon, although I still get the occasional fancy dress request from my now grown-up sons! What followed was a twenty-year career in stitched textiles, teaching machine embroidery and creating textile art. Teaching has certainly always been an important part of what I do, and my work has ranged from teaching C&G in adult education, to running workshops for schoolchildren and disabled adults.

I have been a member of Prism, regularly exhibiting with them at London venues and I'm a long-time participant in Cambridge Open Studios. My work has explored themes of concealment and revelation in particular – I've always been interested in people and their stories.

Recently I've returned to my love of painting and drawing, and my focus has shifted once more. Although I now enjoy painting large acrylic abstracts, I'm also exploring ways of combining my new-found love of painting with stitch. The results are a series of collaged and stitched works on paper. Sometimes abstract, sometimes representational, they are inspired by my surroundings and the landscape, although my love of colour, shape and design provides strong links to previous textile work. It is the constant thrill of what might come next that excites and drives me forward.

www.ginaferrari-art.co.uk
www.facebook.com/GinaFerrariTextileArt
www.facebook.com/GinaFerrariArtist
www.instagram.com/gina_ferrari_art

∧ *Wings to Fly*. My interest with concealment led to research on the artist Frida Kahlo. Frida contracted polio as a child followed by a tragic accident in her late teens. When she lost her leg as a result of gangrene, she wrote in her diary, 'Why do I need feet when I have Wings to Fly?'. These machine embroidered shoes in their decorated box were made in dedication to her courage.

Jessica Grady

I'm a mixed media embroidery artist who is fascinated by colour and materials. I live and work in West Yorkshire UK, and have a small but very colourful studio just outside Leeds. I have a degree in Textiles from Norwich University of the Arts, from which I graduated in 2014. I've worked within the textile design industry and have created embroideries and print designs for various fashion and interior companies, as well as for the film industry. I still undertake a variety of freelance work within commercial print design, but my main practice is now my own art combined with teaching.

I'm particularly drawn to what other people consider to be rubbish – transforming this discarded waste into beautiful embellishments which are hand-stitched onto fabric. I create highly detailed, three-dimensional tactile sculptures and wall art, mainly with an abstract focus. My pieces are inspired by their materials or a certain texture or colour within something that I see. I don't tend to plan out my work. Instead, I let my embellished designs evolve naturally by working in layers of intricate detail, adding decorative hand stitches as a final flair. I want my artwork to evoke curiosity from the viewer; I design pieces so that they reveal more from different viewpoints and angles. I work in lots of saturated, 'zingy' colours that ping off each other, adding flecks of metallic accents and neon pops. All my work is stitched by hand; I enjoy the slow process and gradual building-up of stitches and embellishments. I think it's a great juxtaposition of such a traditional, historical process with a contemporary twist.

∨ *Pulse*. A three-dimensional hand-embellished sculpture created using old silicone sink rings, recycled telephone cables and printed shower-mat sequins. These were hand-stitched onto pink scuba fabric and stretched over a three-dimensional dome shape. This piece was inspired by underwater corals and was designed to reflect colourful sea anemones and flowing seaweed strands.

I'm a member of the textile group Art Textiles: Made in Britain. We're an exhibiting group of professional artists and have had showcase exhibitions at various arts venues and shows across the UK and beyond, including the Festival of Quilts in Birmingham, UK. I was also invited as an ambassador for the group to the 2020 19th Tokyo International Great Quilt Festival in Japan.

Alongside exhibiting and selling my work, I also teach workshops to various schools, colleges, universities, groups and guilds across the UK and abroad. I'm very passionate about teaching and infusing the younger generation, particularly with a love for creating and stitch. I lecture about my creative practices and the various techniques and ideas of recycling and sustainability.

I'm a member of my local Embroiderers' Guild and lead their Young Embroiderers Group. Showing children and young adults that textiles and embroidery is great for mental health and creativity is very important and something I fully intend to explore and continue.

In 2018, I was awarded the Embroiderers' Guild 18–30 Scholarship, which gave me the opportunity to have an individual gallery space at the Knitting and Stitching Shows in London and Harrogate UK, together with a bursary for purchasing new equipment and materials to develop my practice. This was an invaluable experience which helped with my confidence as an embroidery artist, as well as providing many trickle-down opportunities from which I am still reaping the benefits, several years down the line.

In the future I'm keen to keep pushing the boundaries of what can be stitched onto fabric – in my mind, anything is possible!

www.jessicagrady.co.uk
@jessica_rosestitch
www.facebook.com/watch/jessicagradyembroideryartist

∧ Textile swatch samples.

Nikki Parmenter

I have always been creative and my enthusiasm for the arts resulted in my enrolling on an Art Foundation course. I achieved a First Class BA Honours Degree and an MA in Fine Art, specialising in painting. After taking a year out, I undertook a teaching qualification at Goldsmiths College in London. I taught for 30 years at Poynton High School, Cheshire UK, in the posts of art teacher and Head of Art. In 2016, I left full-time work and am now positively relishing the fact that I can plan my own agenda. This includes supply teaching and developing my own work through exhibitions, talks and workshops. I'm a member of Textile 21, Cheshire Artists' Network, the Wirral Society of Arts and Glossop Embroiderers' Guild.

I have a husband, two grown-up children, three dogs and a house full of artwork and related stuff – not clutter but creative potential!

Throughout my teaching career I continued to produce my artwork, creating mainly paper pieces. I've always been interested in different times and cultures, mythology and symbolism and I base my imagery around these themes. At the suggestion of my husband (a sculptor and ex-head of the Art Foundation course at Tameside College) I progressed from using paper to cutting compositions from plywood and MDF. This proved to be an interesting development but I felt that the wood was a somewhat inflexible material to use. A chance encounter with Margaret Beal's book *Fusing Fabric* triggered my fascination with manipulating textiles and inspired the purchase of my first sewing machine.

∧ *Marine Magic*, 12in (30cm) diameter. This piece was created using a variety of techniques and media. Embroidery thread was wrapped around a copper flower-arranging hoop to create a spider's web. The fish, seahorse and turtle were drawn onto calico and pinned onto funky foam before being hand embroidered and padded. Seaweed was cut from funky foam, with added hand stitching, acrylic paint and tiny split pins. I stitched onto water-soluble fabric to create organic forms and wrapped pipe cleaners to look like fronds. Using shibori, beads were tied onto iridescent fabric.

Over the years I've developed a mixed media/ textiles/recycling approach to my work, whilst still exploring my chosen themes. I have turned into a magpie, collecting all manner of materials including unusual items such as hosepipes, car wheel trims, plastic tubing, as well as more conventional media. I enjoy the challenge of incorporating unexpected materials into my work.

My work is often made on a large scale and as it can take several months to complete each piece I am reluctant to part with them. As a result, the walls in my house are adorned with colourful images and the garage houses some of my earlier pieces. I don't have a particular favourite piece but I am always striving to make sure that each project is more successful than the last.

In terms of advice for creating your own mixed media work, I would encourage you to just go for it and tackle a piece on a larger scale with different media. I also act upon a saying – *more is more* – as I am prone to work on every square centimetre of the image surface!

I provide talks, demonstrations and workshops to various groups, schools and societies and I have exhibited widely as an individual and as part of a group. I have written a number of articles and projects for different magazines and am a visiting tutor at the Janome Sewing School, supported by Janome with the use of their sewing machines to produce my work.

www.nikkiparmenterartworks.com
www.facebook.com/nikkiparmenterartworks

∧ *Underwater World*, 10½ x 16in (27 x 41cm). This piece uses the same entrapment method as *Tulipmania*. I layered fabrics and cellophane between the PVC, positioning them to form an arch. Free machine embroidery created seaweed, coral and shell forms. Seaweed made from funky foam was stuck to the surface with beads. The fish was produced by tracing the outline onto PVC. A soldering iron was used to burn decorative holes through the plastic.

Kate Wells

I didn't set out to make lace. It arrived in my studio by a process of serendipity, a feel for a new direction that somehow brought together a lifetime of treasures – medieval goldsmiths' work, early Renaissance paintings, gilded frames and enamelled reliquaries, Italian and French lace. A visit to the Burrell Collection in Glasgow, Scotland, took my breath away, standing in the presence of rolls of 18th-century hand-made lace. When I received an invitation to take part in an exhibition called 'Festival of Spirit' in 2010, all these 'sparks' came together and I began to sample, creating a small collection of precious lace work called *Fragments of Splendour*.

At Loughborough College of Art & Design, where I took my embroidery degree in 1973–76, sampling was never my strength. I always visualised the finished piece of work and then produced it, so to speak. Whilst at Manchester Polytechnic (now MMU) for my MA in Textiles, Judy Barry introduced me to the industrial 'Irish' machine; I was hooked. My first direction was to stitch landscapes on large canvases, the half-inch swing of the needle making it easy to draw freely with broad stitches. I filled sketchbooks travelling up and down from my teaching at the Art School in Glasgow to my home in Sheffield, and responded to the very different Scottish environment and the gritty, textural Scottish school of painters. Early years of exhibiting with the 62Group were exciting, showing in Japan and having two pieces of work purchased by the Museum of Modern Art in Kyoto. Family life brought along two daughters and, with regular commissions, I spent hours at the machine making large landscapes and painted hangings – notably for Sheffield University Students' Union.

< *At Your Feet*, 87 x 8in (220 x 21cm). Gold embroidered lace on dissolvable fabric, worked on the industrial 'Irish' machine. Exhibited at Art in Action in 2013, it has been a catalyst for a collection of lace commissions. It came from walking through a beautiful garden early in the morning, over stones and pebbles onto grass and flowers. As a roll of lace, it resonates with Italian and French lace in the Burrell Collection, Glasgow.

From 1984 until 2016, the Art in Action festival (Waterperry House, Oxfordshire) was an important part of my creative year. I was a regular demonstrator and latterly curated the textiles section, bringing together some amazing artists. Showing and sharing skills with ceramicists, jewellers, painters, sculptors, calligraphers and so many more was a nourishment any artist might crave, and it opened up channels of connections. My daughter, Roanna Wells, exhibited in 2009, winning the peer-award, Best of the Best (I was so proud!).

Gradually, 'stitch-drawing' relaxed into black and white, colour into charcoal, large into small, and the work loosened and started to play. This led me to dig deeper into this parallel new language of gold threads, fine silk crepeline and organza and dissolvable fabrics. Like chapters in a book, new themes and subjects open up as life moves on.

I work to commission from my studio in Sheffield.

www.katewellsartist.co.uk

∧ *Tree of Life*, 8 × 10in (20 × 25cm). Gold guipure lace on dissolvable fabric, 'Irish' embroidery. Made for a private commission, the design followed research into 17th-century pattern books, stumpwork caskets and Jacobean formal garden plans.

BOOK EIGHT

WOWbook

Guest Editor
Lynda Monk

8

Welcome to WOWbook 8
BOOK EIGHT

Well, we certainly have plenty of variety in this eighth WOWbook. I have really enjoyed the ways our selected artists have worked to produce such brilliant results. Techniques range from making miniature corsets to using a design app to produce some fabulous art. They cover everything from scrolls and book-making (with innovative methods of printing) all the way through to the joys of Tyvek. The secret to using the book is to explore the methods described and then consider how to apply them to your own design sources and ways of working. It's all waiting in the book. We also have an in-depth interview with the ever popular Anne Kelly – there is so much to enjoy.

I was delighted to be asked to write a piece for this book as a tribute to the late Olga Norris. Olga was one of the featured artists in our *Approaches to Stitch: Six Artists* book. I was editor at the time and putting it together had unexpected consequences in that I found such inspiration in the work of all the artists. This was especially true of Olga and I have very fond memories of her and still use some of the design techniques that she employed.

It seems very fitting to have such an exciting section on Tyvek, that great and adaptable non-woven insulation material. I was early in adopting this useful material after it was shown to me by one of the participants on an in-service (INSET) textile teacher training course many years ago. I ran courses and wrote numerous books based on it but I'm pretty sure that the Tyvek crown has since passed to Lynda Monk with all the wonderful additional techniques she has discovered.

We have been very fortunate to have had Lynda's services as editor and she has gone to great lengths to find us the unusual, the artistic and the most colourful textile artists for the last five WOWbooks. Sourcing articles, explaining what is needed, checking and editing the results of the search is a thrilling, but time-consuming, occupation and Lynda now feels the call to get back to her own exciting work and experiments. I am convinced that she will be making some amazing new discoveries and, no doubt will be featuring as one of our future artists.

This book was produced under the restrictions of the UK lockdown but I think all the artists featured – who overcame great difficulties in sourcing their materials, developing all their ideas, producing great articles and getting their work to us – have done a magnificent job. To all of them, to Lynda herself, Michael Wicks whose photography continues to be second to none, and Fiona Edwards who makes it all happen: I raise a glass and say a big THANK YOU. It's a great book.

Maggie Grey

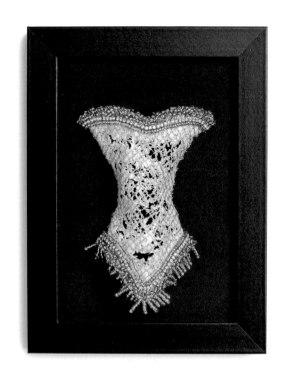

∧ Fran Holmes' mini corset made from white Lutradur overlaid with a gold synthetic net. A trim of gold seed beads is clustered along the top edge, then a row of rhinestones and a single row of gold beads. The bottom was decorated with clusters of gold seed beads and a fringe made from seed beads with a further row of rhinestones and gold beads added.

> *Quiet Work* by the late Olga Norris. This piece shows Olga's typical use of printing and hand stitching. Her pieces were often more radical and challenging but I love the quiet simplicity that this piece portrays.

FOREVER AUTUMN
A mixed-media landscape

Bev Caleno

I am fascinated by the changing seasons and how sunlight glows through the trees whatever the month; I am also a watercolour painter and have painted similar scenes to this one. It's a popular calming subject reminiscent of walks through the local woods during lockdown. It also makes me think of 'light at the end of the tunnel' reminding us that there are better days ahead.

I have made many samples with Lynda Monk using Tyvek, felt and Bondaweb fusible webbing. After playing around, I discovered that I could create abstract trees. Seeing the serendipity of how painted Tyvek creates a silver birch effect, I decided I wanted to make something more representational, which gave the effect of light coming through the trees. I changed the fabric and materials, using velvet instead of felt, but kept the Tyvek effect and was really excited by the way it turned out, reminding me of trees and creating lovely soft edges. My aim was to create an artwork that looks like a painting but, when you look closely, you can see some of the fabric and stitches.

MATERIALS

- A piece of 10 x 14in (25.5 x 35cm) (approx.) white or cream velvet
- Iron-on Vilene 250
- Acrylic inks in lemon yellow, blue, orange and sepia
- Acrylic or fabric metallic paints (Lumiere work well, if you have them)
- Black acrylic or fabric paint
- Tyvek fabric
- Bondaweb fusible webbing
- Green and brown organza
- Misty Fuse fusible web
- Small scraps of green, grey, gold or patterned sheer fabric or silks
- Cotton bobbin or overlocking thread in black or grey

OPTIONAL

- Green machine embroidery thread
- Foil and/or magic dots

EQUIPMENT

- Baking paper
- 4 spray or pump spray bottles
- Credit card
- Paintbrush
- Paint palette
- Iron
- Sewing machine with free motion embroidery foot
- Rotary cutter, mat and ruler

∧ My finished piece
Winter Sunlit Beech.

The painty bit

In this first session, we'll be creating the painted background.

1. Add a few drops of different coloured acrylic ink into your spray bottles. You can use the pump-style bottles available from art shops or the small spray bottles you can buy from chemists. Both give the desired effect. Add water to about a third of the way up and give it a little shake. You can test the colour on a piece of scrap fabric but remember it will dry a little bit lighter.

2. Lay the piece of cut velvet fabric on a protective cover. I have suggested a piece 10 × 14in (25.5 × 35cm) as this provides you with enough of a border to produce a finished artwork of 8 × 12in (20 × 30cm) which will fit nicely in to a standard 16½ × 12in (42 × 30cm) frame with a 2in (5cm) mount.

3. Turn your fabric around to work landscape. About two-thirds up and in the centre, spray a halo of the lemon yellow ink, then spray an orange halo around the yellow.

4. Taking your blue ink, spray the whole piece except over the orange and yellow sunshine.

5. Spray the foreground with sepia ink – you can afford to go quite dark with this.

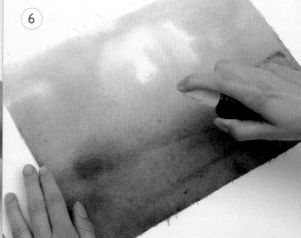

6. Add some darker tones here and splat some neat ink in as well. Try to avoid the blue sky at the top.

7. Using the thicker black fabric paint, squirt out a small amount onto a plate or palette. Dip the edge of your credit card into the paint and, roughly where the horizon is, make little upright marks to depict trees in the distance. This can be done when the fabric is still damp and will give softer marks.

8. Repeat the marks with the credit card when the velvet has dried and you will get harder, sharper lines.

9. Using the metallic fabric paints, paint your pieces of Tyvek. The paint should be watered down – just a little, so the paint is still quite thick. Let it blend in and paint both sides.

10. When your Tyvek is dry, cut it into random strips horizontally. Make sure most of them are a little bit longer than your velvet background, with a maximum width about 1 in (2.5cm) and a minimum of ¼ in (0.5cm).

11. Leave everything to dry.

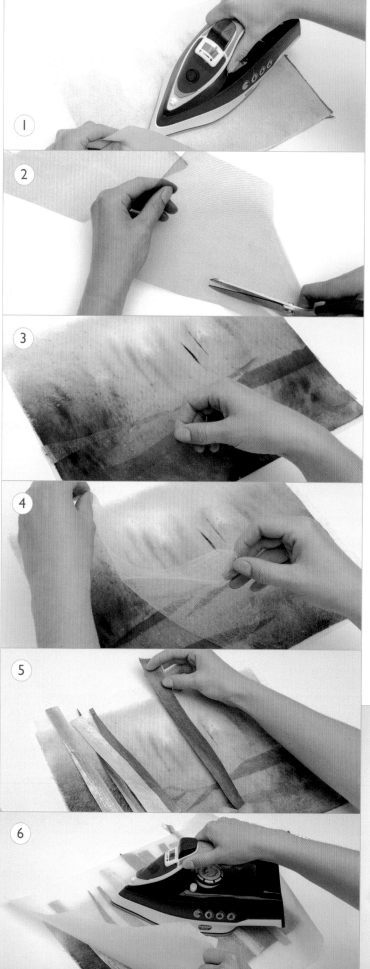

The sticky bit

In this next section, we will be building up the background and applying the Tyvek strips.

1. Iron the Vilene onto the back of the velvet. This is very important as it gives extra stability.

2. Cut a few strips of coloured organza in long tapered shapes.

3. Lay them on the velvet background. You can achieve an interesting aerial perspective by laying the smaller pieces towards the horizon.

4. Carefully lay the Misty Fuse over the velvet, ensuring it covers all the edges.

5. Arrange your painted strips of Tyvek on top of the Misty Fuse. Try not to over-think this but do consider that smaller trees will be further back. Overlap and place a few at a slight angle.

6. Set your iron to a medium heat. Place a piece of baking paper over the whole piece of work. Using a little pressure, glide the iron over your piece. The Tyvek will start melting away creating an interesting effect.

7. Take your time with this. Keep checking by lifting the baking paper. If you keep the iron on for too long or if it is too hot, too much of the Tyvek will burn away. Too little heat or pressure and the Tyvek won't burn away at all or stick to the background.

8. Set your iron to cool. Taking your foil with the right side facing up, use the edge of the iron to make little marks to add smaller tress or branches. You could also add some hot spots and foil on the tree trunks for a bit of extra sparkle.

The stitchy bit

For this last section, we are going to add stitch.

I have used free motion embroidery to create this piece. To set up your sewing machine, lower the feed dogs and attach the free motion foot. I use a fine cotton, bobbin thread or overlocking cotton to avoid stitching heavy lines.

The weight of lines in machine embroidery art can be very tricky, as it is difficult to achieve a soft, blended or broken line. This can sometimes result in very heavy, outlined artwork. With this piece, I am trying to achieve a sketchy look so that the stitches are only noticed on close inspection.

1. Sew up and down the tree trunks. Try to get a fairly consistent stitch length. This will secure all the trees to the background. Don't worry too much about sewing exactly on the Tyvek strips as this will all add to the loose effect.

2. Lay out some small pieces of silk and organza on a cutting board. I have used silvers and golds to give a winter feel but multicoloured, patterned fabric works really well too. Use a rotary cutter and ruler to make snippets of fabric.

3. Arrange these tiny pieces over the trees, where the leaves should be. Remember, these will stick to the Misty Fuse where the Tyvek has burnt away. You can add more small pieces of Misty Fuse if you would like a heavier covering of leaves.

4. Place the baking paper over your work and carefully iron, using the cool setting or the Tyvek will shrivel. Iron the areas where you have added your snippets.

5. Take your work back to your sewing machine and sew sweeping curved lines for branches, catching in the snippets to secure them as you go.

6. Take some of the silk and organza to make shapes around the bottom of the tree trunks. Sew around the leaves to form tiny petal shapes to create the snowdrops. You could use a thicker coloured thread to add more detail in the foreground. This will enhance the feeling of perspective.

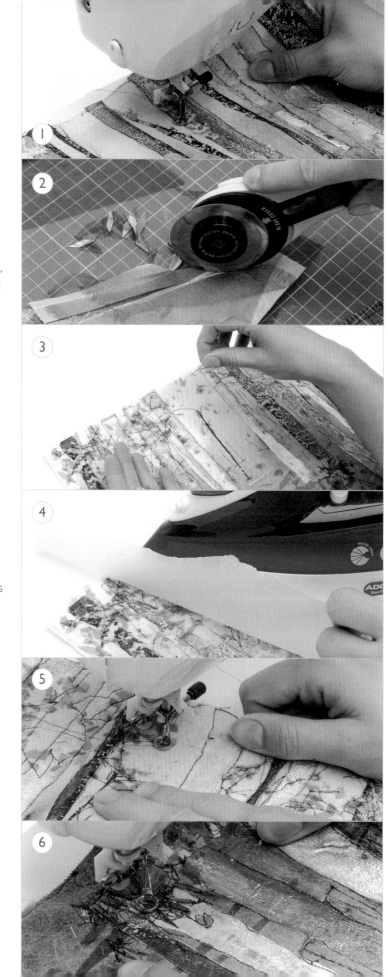

Finishing

When my piece is finished, I frame it using a standard sized 16 × 12in (40 × 30cm) frame.

I don't stretch these pieces but place them within a neutral but not stark white mount, and fix with double-sided tape. I enjoy displaying my pieces behind glass as it gives the feeling of a painting.

Taking it further

You could try changing the season. My work here leaned towards an autumn and winter theme but you could also make spring and summer beech trees with brighter and thicker coverings of snippets, and more foliage and flowers in the foreground.

You could also try changing the format and making it a portrait piece. The stitching could be endless but I prefer to keep a simplicity to the work and rely on strong tonal values to make striking artwork. Both these pieces sold in our exhibition; I also have had several requests for commissions.

∧ > *Autumnal Trees* and *Winter Sun*. Finished pieces ready to mount and frame.

TIP
Decide the size right from the start — working to a standard size will save you time and money.

PARADOX LOST

Maggie Grey discusses the work of the late Olga Norris

∧ *Hot Novel.* This piece brilliantly conveys the compulsion generated by a good book – even at the bus stop. The crows are the chorus of gossip and idle chat. Olga was never one for that and the reader is absorbed and impervious to their noise. The background and the clothing of the figure are closely worked using running stitch.

The late Olga Norris, who sadly died in 2019, was a much respected textile artist whose art-based work was rooted in simple running stitch. This resulted in intricate pieces, often depicting mono-printed outline shapes with a background enhanced by hand stitching. The 'paradox' of the title above refers to the contradictory nature of Olga's work, where the simplicity of the stitching contrasted with the complex nature of the idea or concept that the piece portrayed. The ideas behind her work were anything but simple; many of her designs were produced using image programs. She once told me that her two most important tools were her computer and her hands.

I first met Olga when I was editing a multi-artist book for d4daisy Books in 2013. For me, *Approaches to Stitch* was a fun book, giving me free-rein to select six artists whose work was sufficiently different to offer new ideas, but also harmonious in outcome to result in a good-looking book. In an effort to achieve as broad an approach as possible, we included overseas artists such as Ro Bruhn from Australia and Beryl Taylor from the USA (originally from the UK), both artists I had long admired.

Olga was an inspired choice and our mutual interest in computer design gave us plenty to chat about. She developed a design-led stitching technique which was based on figures, either drawn and scanned or digitally drawn on screen. She approached all her work with a view to setting and solving design problems in order to create a means of expression. She once said to me that she never considered herself a craftsperson and I do think that a better description of her approach to any of her pieces would be that she was a top-flight artist with total command of her craft. For Olga, the craft was a means to an end. She was never obsessed with perfecting her work; it was how she could use it that mattered. She was always experimenting with different approaches and techniques to find additional means of expression. It was the meaning in the image that mattered.

> *Juggler, Red.* Olga's work was generally fairly muted in tone but she sometimes gave us a really colourful reminder that she could 'do colour' in a truly vibrant manner. In this piece, the use of mono-printing and a stitched central figure is given a whole new treatment in vibrant hot colours.

I talked to her husband, Nigel, about Olga's work. He said, 'She was a total original. Even when drawing on external influences, she absorbed and adapted them into the many other inputs that went into her work. Her working practice was very intuitive and subconscious. She would work deliberately and purposefully in developing the design, but the key steps depended on intuition. She would have a number of ideas in development at any one time, and work was often put aside until the ideas crystallised. She often said that she couldn't always explain the reasoning for an image – that was just the way it came out of the creative process.'

Broadly, the work fell into two categories: ideas inspired by her razor-sharp observation of the world, most especially of human interaction and body language; and, more directly, personal pieces that were based on her own emotional experiences. Much of the work is autobiographical.

Olga's work often showed figures in outline only. The background, usually painted or digitally printed, provided the colour and outlined the figures, which sometimes remained unstitched. This technique allowed them to stand out against that heavily stitched background, hand-stitched with running stitch in a manner reminiscent of Kantha stitching. Although the figures were seemingly simple outline drawings, they were able to convey a wealth of information – movement, mood, or a sense of mystery that pushed the viewer into asking questions – wondering what was going on.

> *The Siren Song of Solitude.* As a teenager, Olga wanted to learn to play the saxophone, but her parents would not allow it. Later in life, Olga and Nigel were regulars at jazz concerts. Here, the player has the joy and escape of pure self-expression. Nigel says that it's a very personal piece – she gave it to a friend before she died. In the last few years, Olga had been freed from other responsibilities and been able to devote herself to her art and he likes to think that it represents how she felt in that period.

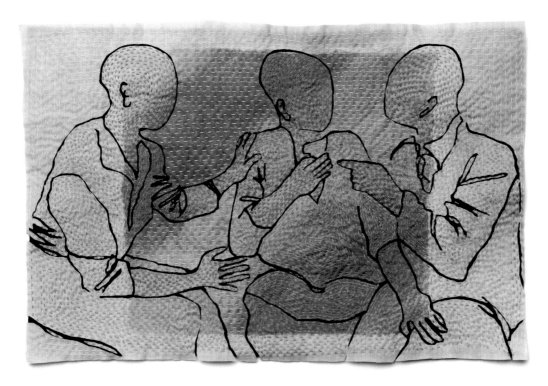

Her work frequently captured a moment in time, resulting in thought-provoking stories which sometimes followed a theme. For instance, *Animated Exchange* shows three figures talking, with particular attention drawn to the body language shown in the hand gestures. The figures are certainly animated, the hands moving vigorously. In the follow-up, *Fates*, the hands tell us that the points having been made, the folk are now considering the new perspectives offered. The central figure is obviously ticking off the points in favour of their arguments and I wonder if it is pure chance that the background stitching, floating across the faces, shows what could be a pair of 'evil' eyes for this character.

< *Fates*. Always fascinated by how gestures are interpreted, Olga had fun concocting this one with its ambiguities.

Olga had been taught to stitch as a child in Greece, mostly using cross stitch. She was pleased to discover that simple stitches, used as enhancement rather than providing a focal point, combined so well with her experiments in print-making. An accomplished print-maker, she was delighted when she found that she was able to combine that with her simple use of stitch, producing animated work that was capable of telling stories.

Having studied art history and aesthetics at degree level, she told me that she often referred to this study for her designs. These were almost always based on real people and were the inspiration for all her work. It is the

drawings – seemingly so simple – that convey expression, state of mind and movement. Her backgrounds were composed of traditional paint and print techniques, often mono-prints. The figure drawings and the painted backgrounds were then scanned into a paint program and, after adjustment, were ironed onto fabric using transfer paper.

As a child in Greece, Olga loved swimming in the sea. Swimming out away from the shore allowed her to be on her own and to escape from the gaggle of relatives for whom she was expected to perform. She produced a series of figures in her works depicting the sea.

∧ *Sleep Deep*. One of Olga's sea series. The 'tendrils' may be the ripples on the surface of the water (see David Hockney's pool pictures for the influences). The viewer could also see in this a reference to *Ophelia* by Millais.

< Silence Louder Than Noise. The viewer is drawn into this piece by the sense of mystery.

Birds also featured in her work and became a motif running through many of her pieces. She loved watching birds, and the different characters they represented. There is a good deal of symbolism in all the bird images. Olga would say that there wasn't always a specific interpretation and people should see it in their own way. However, many of the references are to her own experience.

∨ *Spillikins.* Members of the crow family appear in several pieces – crows cackle and gossip, are demanding and need attention, criticise and disapprove. Just like some people...

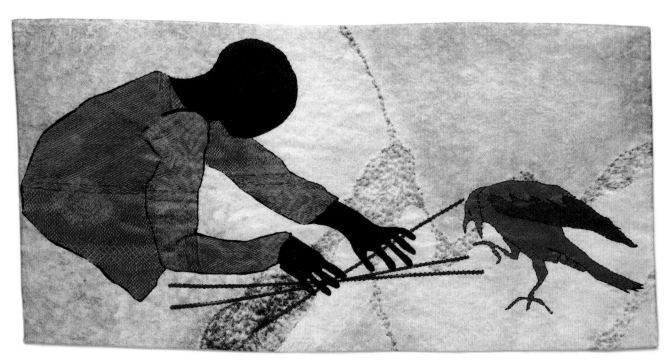

Olga had a great sense of humour, which often crept into her work. Her piece, *Curiosity*, resulted from her sense of the wonder of the universe and how little we know about it. Her rationale for including the cat was because cats are also curious and largely unknowable.

Nigel told me that there were a couple of triggers for this piece. 'We watched a series of Horizon programmes on cosmology. We also had a discussion about science vs arts, and how they are seen. I'm a scientist by training and I tried to explain that science, and especially the kind of mathematics used in cosmology, had a beauty and depth of meaning that rivalled any fine art, but the art world didn't understand that. This was Olga's response (and we always had cats, so apart from the curiosity aspect she would naturally have a cat with her).'

∧ *Curiosity*. Digital image, printed on cotton and hand quilted.

LOVELY LINGERIE
3D mini corsets

Fran Holmes

While studying for my City & Guilds Machine Embroidery Level 3 Diploma, I fell in love with Lutradur/Spunbond. I learnt that it was more versatile than I first expected. What I loved most was the magical way that it changed when heat was applied and as some of the fabric melted away, you were left with a beautiful lace-like effect.

Lutradur/Spunbond is a synthetic fabric that was produced for use in industry. When heat is applied, it does not flame but simply shrinks and melts. It has been used to line the roofs of houses and you could find that it has been used as the base for your bed. Lutradur and Spunbond are, in effect, the same fabric made by different companies. For the textile artist, its qualities are that you can colour it with dye or paint, stitch into it by hand or machine and cut it, either with scissors or using a die cutter machine.

After experimenting with this versatile fabric, I learnt, when using stitch and paint as a resist effect, what happens when heat is applied to shrink and melt the fabric. While most people will paint, stitch and heat distress this fabric, I like to manipulate it to create 3D designs.

Having created an installation of corsets for an exhibition, I decided to design and make a series of mini corsets.

< My completed mini corset created from Lutradur, machine stitched and trimmed with sequins and beads before heat treating to distress.

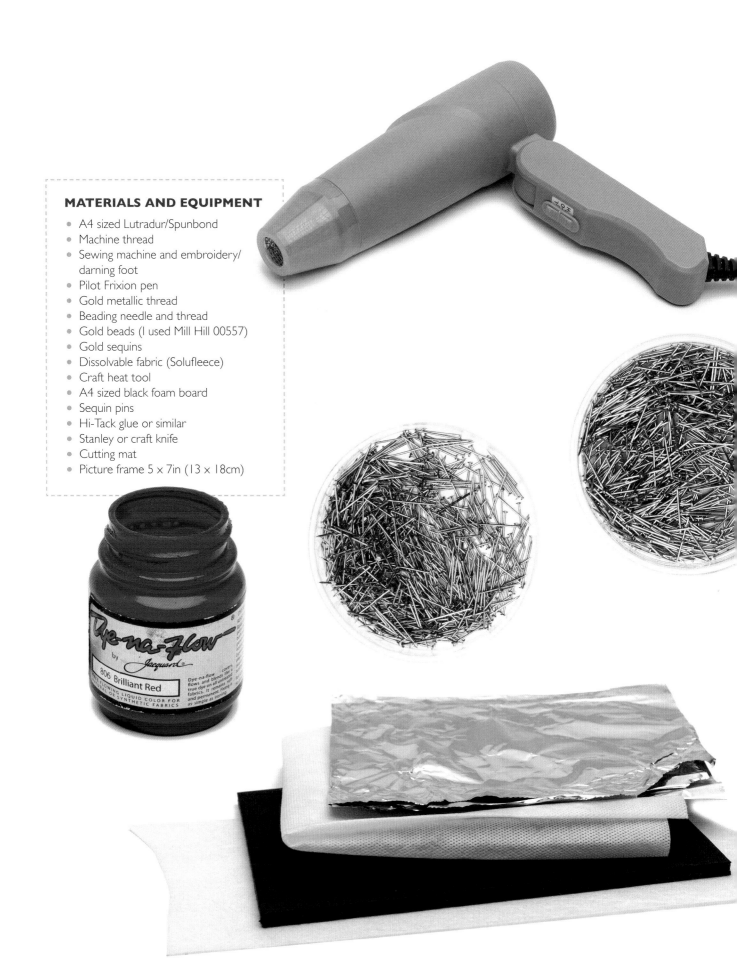

MATERIALS AND EQUIPMENT

- A4 sized Lutradur/Spunbond
- Machine thread
- Sewing machine and embroidery/darning foot
- Pilot Frixion pen
- Gold metallic thread
- Beading needle and thread
- Gold beads (I used Mill Hill 00557)
- Gold sequins
- Dissolvable fabric (Solufleece)
- Craft heat tool
- A4 sized black foam board
- Sequin pins
- Hi-Tack glue or similar
- Stanley or craft knife
- Cutting mat
- Picture frame 5 x 7in (13 x 18cm)

Making your mini corset

1. Make a paper pattern by drawing a corset shape that is no wider than 4in (10cm) at its widest point and no longer than 5in (12.5cm) at its longest point.

2. Pin the template to the Lutradur and carefully cut around.

3. Paint the Lutradur with a liquid dye on both sides and allow to dry. You can leave out this stage if you want a plain white corset. I use Jacquard's Dye-Na-Flow 806 Brilliant Red but you could use Procion dye or Inktense blocks, should you wish. I would recommend that acrylic paint is not used – this adds too much resist to the melting stage when heat is applied. You could experiment with other liquid colours before you continue to stitch.

If you are using other methods of colouring your Lutradur, test any samples you try by soaking in water first to make sure the colour doesn't come out. Allow to dry and then heat with a heat tool to ensure it is colour fast.

4. With your Frixion pen, draw diagonal lines on your corset.

5. Using your sewing machine, stitch along the diagonal lines using gold metallic thread. I used a straight stitch but you could choose an automatic design stitch from your machine, if you wish. Trim off any loose thread.

6. Cut two pieces of Solufleece to 5 x 7in (13 x 18cm) and pin the Lutradur corset between the two pieces of Solufleece. Other types of soluble fabric are available and you could use what you have got, but my preference is always Solufleece.

7. With your Frixion pen, draw a border beyond the top of the corset and beyond the bottom edge of the corset. I used a ruler to measure the distance from the corset to the edge of the border ½in (1.25cm) deep.

TIP
When using a metallic thread, start with a new needle. A metallic 80 or a top stitch needle 90 both work well and cause less frustration with broken thread if this needle is kept solely for this thread.

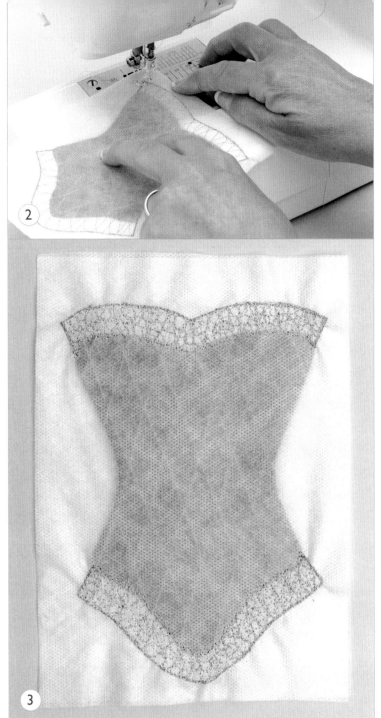

Stitching

1. Using metallic thread in your machine, in free machine embroidery mode, feed dogs down and no stitch length, with a darning foot or embroidery foot, stitch along the line you have drawn on the Solufleece. Starting at one side of the corset with the needle in the corset, stitch away from the corset following the line you have drawn and back down into the corset at the other side, then stitch back along the same line.

2. Now create a wavy stitch line in this border at the top and bottom of the corset by stitching into the corset at the bottom and then into the stitch line at the top of the border. This creates a grid onto which all your other stitches will hang.

3. To create a lacy effect, stitch the border as if you are doodling in circles to fill in the border between the corset and the top stitched line. Remember to keep stitching into the top of the corset and the top stitched line of the border.

4. You can create a denser border by adding more stitching. Too little will result in the border being too loose and this, in turn, may produce holes when the Solufleece is dissolved.

5. When you are happy with your stitching for the top border, repeat the process around the bottom of the corset.

If you are familiar with free machine embroidery you may wish to make a lacy stitch border in a different way.

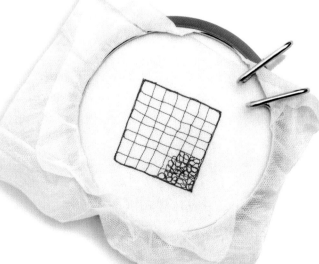

If you are new to free machine embroidery you will find that mastering it is just practice. It is very rewarding when you have mastered the art. If you need to practise the technique first, take a double piece of Solufleece, place in an embroidery frame and draw a box with the Frixion pen. Stitch around the outside twice and then make a grid in the box. Now fill in with a doodling stitch. Trim away your excess Solufleece before soaking the whole piece in warm water until the Solufleece has disappeared. Allow to air dry flat. The stitches should have held together in the square shape you drew.

Dissolving

1. Trim away any excess Solufleece front and back of the corset before soaking in water.

2. Soak the complete corset in warm water until all the Solufleece has dissolved away. You may want to change the water before this process is complete.

3. Allow to dry on a cake cooling rack. Do not dry with heat as you may distort the fabric. You could remove excess water by blotting with kitchen paper if, like me, you are too impatient to wait!

Beading

1. Once the corset is dry, hand stitch gold sequins and beads around the top and bottom of the corset border.

2. Stitch gold beads to the points of the diamond shapes.

Applying heat

Now for the exciting bit – applying heat to shape your corset.

1. First cut out the pattern in paper. The corset pattern measures 3in (7.5cm) across the top, 1in (2.5cm) at the waist and 2in (5cm) across the bottom. The corset is 3½in (9cm) tall.

2. Take the black foam board and place the pattern on it. Cut around the pattern with a Stanley or craft knife, being careful of your fingers! This is the shape you are going to pin to your corset.

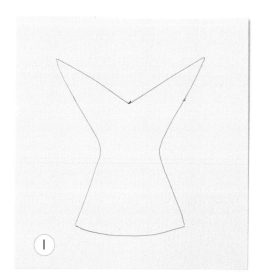

3. Holding the corset in one hand, pinch it in at the waist around the edge of the foam board.

4. Lining-up the points of the foam board with the top of the corset, just below the stitched border, pin both sides in the middle at the waist. Then pin one side at a time. Use approximately five pins for each side. I used gold sequin pins for my piece.

5. Now your corset should be nicely pinched in at the waist and domed, producing a 3D effect. I sometimes use a piece of scrunched up foil to support the shape.

6. When you are happy with the shape of your corset, apply heat to the fabric side with the heat tool on a heatproof surface. When using a heat tool, always work in a well-ventilated room and use breathing apparatus if appropriate for your health.

7. The aim when using a heat tool is to create small holes in the fabric giving a lacy, distressed effect. You cannot be totally in control of where the holes will form but apply heat gradually as you can always go back with more heat if required. You may wish to hold the corset with a wooden barbeque stick to stop it from moving around while you are working.

Do not wave your heat tool around as if you are drying your hair but aim it at the corset and then take it away as soon as you see the fabric shrinking and melting. Then focus on another part of the corset.

8. Some areas of the corset will not melt, while other areas will melt quickly into larger holes. This is because the density of the fabric is not even due to the spun process of its manufacture. Also remember that stitch can act as a resist to the heat.

Do not direct heat at the sequins as they could melt (I haven't found this to be a problem).

9. While the fabric is hot from the heat tool, it's malleable but be careful as you could burn your fingers especially on the metal pins. The fabric cools quickly and then becomes quite firm and will stay in shape.

10. Remove any foil if you have used it.

TIP
Use sequin pins – dressmaking pins are too long for this job.

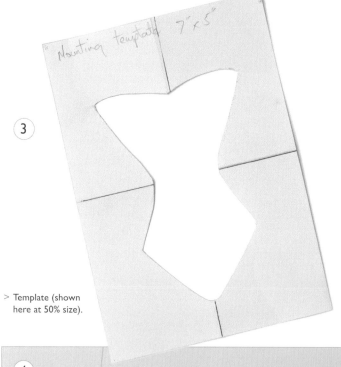

③

> Template (shown here at 50% size).

④

⑤

Framing

All that is left is to frame your corset.

1. Cut a piece of black foam board 5 x 7in (13 x 18cm). This will be the background for your corset. Make sure this foam board fits inside your frame.

2. Cut a piece of paper 5 x 7in (13 x 18cm). Draw central horizontal and vertical lines on the paper.

3. Using the template, cut an aperture in the centre of this piece of paper. This will help you centralise the corset in the middle of the frame.

4. Place the paper template on the foam board and pin at each corner.

5. Apply glue on the back of the corset's foam board and place in the centre of the template. When the glue is dry, remove the pins and lift the paper template off carefully.

6. Place the mounted corset in the frame. Stand back and admire!

> Top left. My finished mini corset.

> Bottom left. This little red corset was adapted from the pattern used in this workshop. The top was modified to enable a turn-down in free machine embroidery. A cord was added to give a laced-up effect.

> Top right. For this corset, Lutradur was dyed black with gold metallic thread for the stitching. A small zigzag stitch was used, with rhinestones added.

> Bottom right. A white corset, stitched and trimmed using the same method as the black one, top right.

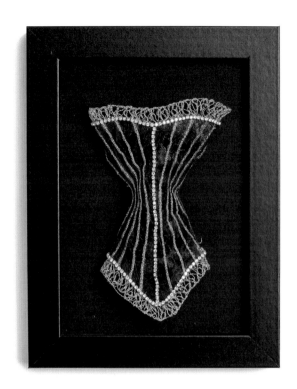
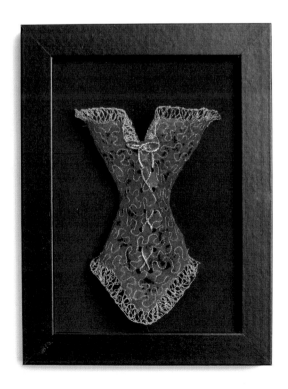
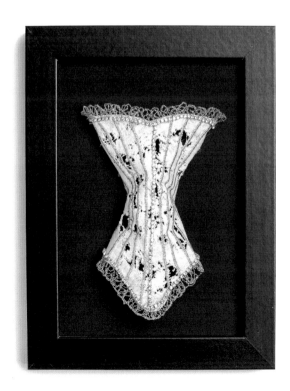

Taking it further

As with anything creative, there are endless possibilities. This workshop has taken you through the process of making one little corset. I'm sure you'll have your own ideas for decorating them.

As you can see, I got carried away and have created a complete installation of corsets! Here are some from my collection.

For some of the corsets, I added a diamante chain, lace or net. The combination of beads, stitch, lace and net are endless.

To create a larger-sized corset, a similar technique can be applied. Instead of forming the corset around foam board, a life-sized mannequin could be used.

The corsets shown here have all been made following the basic pattern in this workshop. By changing the colour and adding different trims, very different effects can be achieved. All the corsets have been treated with a heat tool after the completion of the stitching.

Anne is an award-winning textile artist, author and tutor based in the UK, exhibiting and teaching internationally. Her four books for Batsford represent her project and collaborative work, dealing with themes of nature, folk art, travel and migration. Anne's heavily embroidered fabric collages are reminiscent of tapestry work and her signature stitching technique is applied to a variety of surfaces.

Q In your recent book, *Textile Travels* (published by Batsford and reviewed in the Members' club for *WOWbook 06*), you say that: 'As Artists, travelling helps us to locate our place in the world and share our practice with new audiences'. How had travel prior to the pandemic allowed you to find your place in the world?

A Travelling was mainly for work before the pandemic and it enabled me to see the world. It was wonderful to visit different countries and be shown them through the eyes of like-minded stitchers. I was able to visit Australia, New Zealand and India several times. I am so glad to have been able to work with such inspired and inspiring students.

My last overseas workshop was in America and finished at the end of February 2020. I was fortunate to have been taught a variety of techniques and methods in different countries by experts, as part of my travels which have influenced and informed my work. One such piece is *Europeans*. It is a piece about my family's heritage and includes pictures of my family around a central map of Europe. The words evoke thoughts about our connections with travel and migration. Many of these experiences are documented in my latest book *Textile Travels*.

Q Your work is full of meaning and has a great capacity for telling a story. Was there a tradition for storytelling in your family and how did that establish itself through your artistic interpretations?

A There was no real tradition of storytelling as such but because of my parents' diverse backgrounds, there were always family stories and comparisons about their upbringings to be made at home. My grandmother was a maker and very prolific and I was influenced by that.

> *Europeans*. 39 x 23½in (100 x 160cm). This piece was produced for the 'Well Travelled' exhibition held at the Ruthin Craft Centre, Ruthin, North Wales, UK, in 2021.

∨ Folding fabric book showing found papers and fabric remnants. Anne used her grandmother, a refugee from Nazi Germany, as inspiration for this piece which featured in Anne's workshop '100 Years Haberdashery' in *WOWbook 04*.

∨ *Eastern Embroidery*. Created from a textile sample stitch book gifted to Anne by an embroidery guild.

Q Much of the work you describe incorporates materials, objects, textiles and embroidery that you acquire, whether when on your travels, in a local charity shop or gifted to you by people. How do you catalogue all these items you have and do you become attached to the finished pieces made using these items?

A I am very fortunate in that I receive many items as gifts and am able to judge immediately whether they will be useful for my work or for sharing through workshops. I am quite unattached emotionally to these items – I see them as the means to an end, creating a new piece of work. I am always encouraging my students to make something beautiful from pieces that they have lying around and are not using. I am drawn to pieces that fit a theme that I may be investigating, but rarely buy things 'just in case'. I am always delighted when a piece finds a new home.

< *Unfinished Journey Boat.*
This hand-made canoe
was covered with
textiles and laminated
paper. The design was
made from a pattern
using partially completed
embroidery patterns
on linen and cotton,
and paper transfers. The
pattern was produced in
stages and fitted to the
canoe in sections.

Q You have mentioned *Unfinished Journey Boat*,
Did you find the canoe or did the canoe
find you?

A I was looking for a wooden canoe skeleton
and serendipitously found one on 'Preloved'.
It was in Ripon (North Yorkshire) and I live
in Kent, at the other end of England, so we
hired a van to collect it from the owner,
whose children had made it at school many
years ago. It needed major cleaning but a

wonderful shape emerged from the dirt and
it has been a joy to work on. The covering
was made from a pattern based on partially
completed printed embroidery patterns on
linen and cotton, and paper transfers. These
were gifted to me by a student. The pattern
was produced in stages and fitted to the
skeleton in sections. It was separated into
two parts to make it easier to transport,
which screw together.

Q With this in mind, how do you transition to work on larger-scale items and is it a challenge moving from small pieces to the behemoths of a full-sized garden shed or canoe?

A Oddly enough, I find the larger items, once they are designed, easier to complete. After deciding on a theme and gathering together the materials, the pieces are quite straightforward. I am often asked 'how long does it take' to complete a piece, and the answer is that the making is not the hardest part. Planning and designing are more time consuming and I find smaller work quite challenging as a result. This year I have made and sold many pieces of work online. People seem to appreciate and enjoy original art work.

∧ Full-sized shed on wheels, re-covered with book pages and maps, fabric and embroidery and exhibited at Knitting and Stitching Shows in London, Dublin and Harrogate.

< Vintage haberdashery box repurposed for themed embroidery and mixed media work. Anne produced this '100 Years Haberdashery' workshop for WOWbook 04.

∨ Maud's House. Textile wallhanging. 43 x 43in (110 x 110cm). A homage to artist Maud Lewis. This piece was drawn with fabric pens and Indian printing blocks. The images decorating the house were based on Maud Lewis's designs and the whole piece was overstitched. It was exhibited around the UK including at the Knitting and Stitching Shows.

Q Your books include a variety of objects that you have altered and embellished in order to tell a story. Has the use of everyday objects been something that has facilitated your themes and how do you think they help communicating these?

A Yes, I think that is right. We are surrounded by everyday objects which can become extraordinary when they are altered with textiles and embellishment. People of all ages can connect to objects in different ways, for example a dolls' house is universally loved by all ages but for a variety of reasons.

Q House and home themes are present in your work whether through collage, covered dolls' and bird houses, full-sized sheds or in your workshops. Did you find that during the pandemic, this theme featured strongly in your work and teaching?

A This theme has been a constant and is a popular workshop topic. I use old domestic textiles to work with and they often find their way into pieces based on house and home. During the past year and the lockdowns, our homes have become even more significant and meaningful and I've used them symbolically in new work as a reference to that.

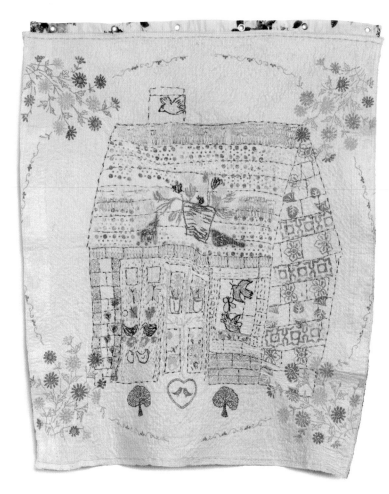

Q Some of us may have travelled more locally during the lockdowns of 2020-21. *Textile Travels* encourages the reader to look at their own travels and history, and what's on their doorstep, rather than solely on physical travel in the present. How did the theme of 'mapping' shape your teaching courses to students during this time, with remote teaching a necessity?

A The theme of mapping your local environment is a part of *Textile Travels*, so it was a natural development during lockdown to investigate this further. My 'Nature Stitch Book' workshops were developed using a lovely gifted tablecloth which I used as a teaching tool and I have also made work using local plants and 'park walk' books for my exhibition 'Well Travelled' at the Ruthin Craft Centre, Ruthin, North Wales, UK in 2021. Students were very keen to develop themes close to home and although online teaching is challenging at first, it is very rewarding and has been a life saver for many during the pandemic. I like to explore the ideas of maps, physical and emotional, and to include them in project work.

∧ Sketchbook pages created as part of nature and park walks to map the local area and note the flora and fauna of the surroundings.

∨ Sketchbook pages using the local area and a haberdashery shop as a theme for exploration and mapping.

< *100 Years War Stories Heart; 1918 Northern Ontario Men in France* heart. This was inspired by northern Ontario men who fought in France in 1918, and the families they left behind.

Q Do you have a standard practice of developing new pieces of work? What is your relationship with a sketchbook? Do you prefer to share techniques when writing/teaching but keep the development of your ideas separate to this?

A I work with, not from sketchbooks. I am always telling my students to make samples before they begin – but I don't! I tend to use my sketchbooks as scrapbooks and I don't copy religiously from them, rather using them as repositories for inspiring ephemera, photos and sketches. It can often be a scrap or small snippet that inspires a whole piece. I do tend to work in series and I suppose that is a form of sampling. I have mood boards and inspirational objects around me in my studio and office. There will be a selection of sketchbooks in my Ruthin show which I hope will shed some light on the creative process.

Blue Book was created on several levels. It is a book about a journey from Kent to Norwich Cathedral. The pages were taken from a farm ledger in northern Ontario and incorporated work for the '100 Hearts' project to commemorate 100 years since the end of the First World War.

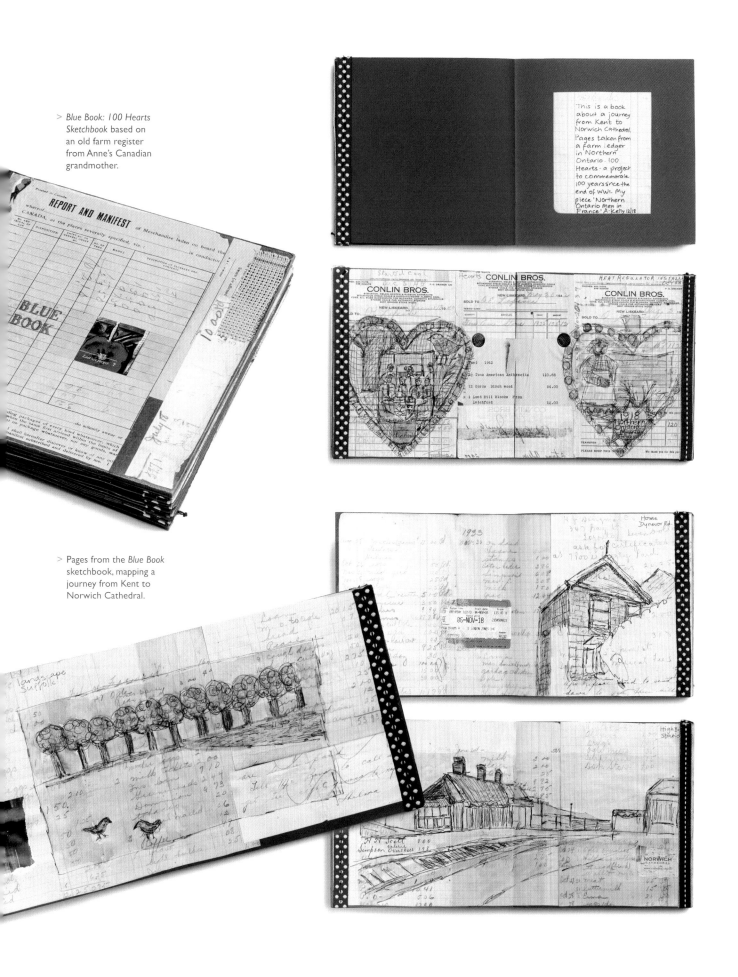

> *Blue Book: 100 Hearts Sketchbook* based on an old farm register from Anne's Canadian grandmother.

> Pages from the *Blue Book* sketchbook, mapping a journey from Kent to Norwich Cathedral.

< *Horse* (left) and *Dog* (right). Each 8½ x 8½in (22 x 22cm). Two portraits exhibited in the 'Isolated Observations' exhibition at the Candida Stevens Gallery in Chichester, West Sussex, UK. These pieces are painted on fabric with casein tempera, and embellished with hand and machine embroidery. The inspiration for these pieces was family members recounting stories of dreams and home during the national Covid lockdown.

Q You have been prolific during lockdown on social media. Have you found that this has been beneficial to you for keeping in touch with followers of your art and to keep a line of communication open for the production of the art you sell?

A Like it or loathe it, social media is an integral part of communicating with students and supporters of my practice. It has been heartening and very encouraging to have sold many small pieces of work during the pandemic I was also able to help my local food bank by donating 10% of sales to them. I have enjoyed sending the work around the world and receiving such positive feedback from recipients.

In 2020, the work I exhibited included portraits as part of the 'Isolated Observations' exhibition at the Candida Stevens Gallery in Chichester, West Sussex, UK. There were four pieces in total: *Dog, Bird, Horse* and *Gloves*. These pieces were painted on fabric with casein tempera, and then stitched and embellished with hand and machine embroidery. This work was inspired by family members recounting stories of dreams and home during the first part of the national lockdown due to the Covid pandemic.

Q You teach classes on a variety of themes, from seaside to home, and walking in nature to birds. Do you like to have a catalogue of the classes you run and how do you go about developing a class to teach? Does the venue's location guide you in a theme, such as a seaside theme when at the coast?

A I have a list of copyrighted classes which I revise and develop annually. Generally, a venue selects from these but occasionally I will suggest a course that particularly suits a specific group or place.

For example, my 'Moving Memories' class is intended to make a meaningful repository for a place special to the maker (which can be real or imagined). I use techniques such as printing, fabric collage, fabric and paper lamination with hand and machine stitching taken from my book *Textile Folk Art*. We make a larger 3D piece and a smaller folding piece as part of the course. As a teaching sample, I made *Dress 1* as part of a series of small pieces based on travel and memory.

In another course I call 'Travels in Textiles', we work from collections of ephemera such as old postcards, receipts, brochures and other papers. These are used to create a folding book or a collaged piece.

< *Dress 1*. 8 x 11in (21 x 29cm) for Anne's 'Moving Memories' course.

∨ *Red Birds*. 21½ x 6in (55 x 15cm). Folding book created for Anne's 'Travels in Textiles' workshop, produced for the 'Well Travelled' exhibition.

The aim is to make a personal response to a special place or event with stitch, drawing and collage. Each participant has their own response and approach, and I often post these on social media to demonstrate how differently we all see the world. My *Red Birds* folding book started out as a teaching sample and was developed using these techniques, with a focus on drawing and stitching in my studio.

Q Your 'Well Travelled' exhibition at the Ruthin Craft Centre and your exhibition at West Dean College in 2021 had been subject to delays and changes, but you were able to attend Ruthin in person as restrictions eased. How did you find the experience of seeing your work and the visitors in person? Does the prospect of exhibiting again create a sense of excitement about the future of exhibiting your work?

A It was very emotional and rewarding to get such positive feedback from visitors who also enjoyed the novel experience of visiting in person. It was an immensely proud moment especially to visit the Ruthin Craft Centre to see it with my family.

I am very excited about exhibiting in 'real life' again! I had temporarily forgotten how much work goes into the preparation for an exhibition. It is huge and exhausting and I am not sure how I ever did it! I think that the pandemic has given us a chance to think of new platforms for art, online and in hybrid settings. I feel especially with textiles that they need to be seen up close and I am very ready to enjoy some real exhibitions, as I am sure everyone is. We have been somewhat deprived culturally during this period, although in the grand scheme of things it was necessary. I think it has made us re-evaluate our priorities and hopefully appreciate anew the role of creativity in our lives.

Q You have work at several exhibitions abroad this year – the Society for Embroidered Work (SEW) in Rome and Pour l'Amour du Fil in Nantes, France. Can you tell us about these exhibitions and the work you are exhibiting? Did it help to have something to work towards?

A I still feel that travelling abroad or sending work outside of the UK is complicated. I was invited to be a guest artist at Pour l'Amour du Fil in 2019 and it was rescheduled three times. However, we were lucky that it did eventually take place at the end of

< Installations from the 'Well Travelled' exhibition which took place at Ruthin Craft Centre in Wales, 28 May–17 July 2021. Photos by Anne Kelly.

September 2021 and I was able to attend, exhibit my work and teach several mini workshops. I showed a range of work inspired by French brocante.

The SEW exhibition is arranged by the Society's organisers, Emily Tull and Cat Frampton, and I am exhibiting a piece called *Undersea Mobile*, inspired by seaside plants and shells. *Undersea Mobile* came out of my original piece, *Undersea*, reflecting on the events of 2020. During the pandemic, I started to work for my local Adult Education service, but on Zoom – not in person. This enabled me to connect with students all over the UK and it was great because it made me work on bi-weekly themes, one of which was the seaside. We looked at coral and shells and some of the central parts of *Undersea* started life as teaching samples. I added some vintage silk from a scarf which had holes in it. I also added some printed pieces of fabric on denim, which began to dictate the darker colourway and jewel-like elements. I was gifted a lovely tablecloth which I used as a border. *Undersea Mobile* was a development of the original piece but created on a smaller scale. Both used textile collage and were created as separate pieces but worked on in the same way – from the front and back using embroidery hoops.

It was great to have exhibitions to work towards during the lockdown – it was wonderful that I was part of these two, as they went ahead as planned.

< *Undersea* based on a seaside theme using a vintage silk scarf and printed pieces of fabric on denim. The border was a gifted tablecloth. *Undersea* was shown in the 'Well Travelled' exhibition and was developed further into *Undersea Mobile*.

∧ *Undersea Mobile*. A smaller piece created out of *Undersea* using textile collages and produced as separate pieces using embroidery hoops.

ONE AT A TIME
Mono-printing for stitch

Sheila Mortlock

I have always liked texture, surfaces that make me want to put out my hand to touch and experience the amazing variety of surfaces to which we are exposed every day. The tactile quality of fabric is definitely one of the reasons why I chose to study printed textiles. I enjoy using printed or painted visual texture and some of my work explores how visual texture can be created with print – yet the printed surface remains a piece of fabric that can be stitched and suitable for many projects.

Mono-printing is a very accessible printing process that anyone can enjoy at home without the necessity for expensive equipment. As the name suggests, it doesn't produce a series of identical results (as happens with digital printing or screen printing limited editions), but allows users to develop textures and surfaces easily and effectively. These can be starting points for stitch and can also be useful for creating textured collage papers for many uses.

For these purposes, however, it is important to print in layers. Not just one layer of colour but building it up until all the background white is hidden; subtleties of colour and pattern are achieved as layers build one on top of another. This takes at least three layers of printing but quite subtle effects can be achieved as print marks sit on top of each other, layer on layer.

The beauty is that no two results will be exactly the same. I have worked on more than one piece of fabric with the same colours, and mostly the same marks and finished with similar but quite different results. For me, that is a bonus and offers exciting possibilities.

MATERIALS AND EQUIPMENT

- White cotton fabric – I use a medium- to heavy-weight fabric as it has to be able to take a few layers of paint, plus collaged fabric and stitch later in the process
- A4 acetate sheet, a laminated sheet of paper or a Gelli plate to use as your printing plate
- Roller/brayer
- Acrylic paints, brushes, sponges
- Textile medium to use with the acrylic paints – there are various manufacturers such as Liquitex, Golden and Colourcraft
- Oil pastels, artists' chalks, pencils, marker pens
- Mark making tools: old store card, kebab stick, found objects etc
- Textural surfaces: bubblewrap, corrugated cardboard, old lace, relief surfaces, etc
- Stencils and small print screens (if you have some)
- Fabrics to collage, including sheer fabrics, and bonding tissue
- Threads for hand and/or machine and other embellishments of your choice

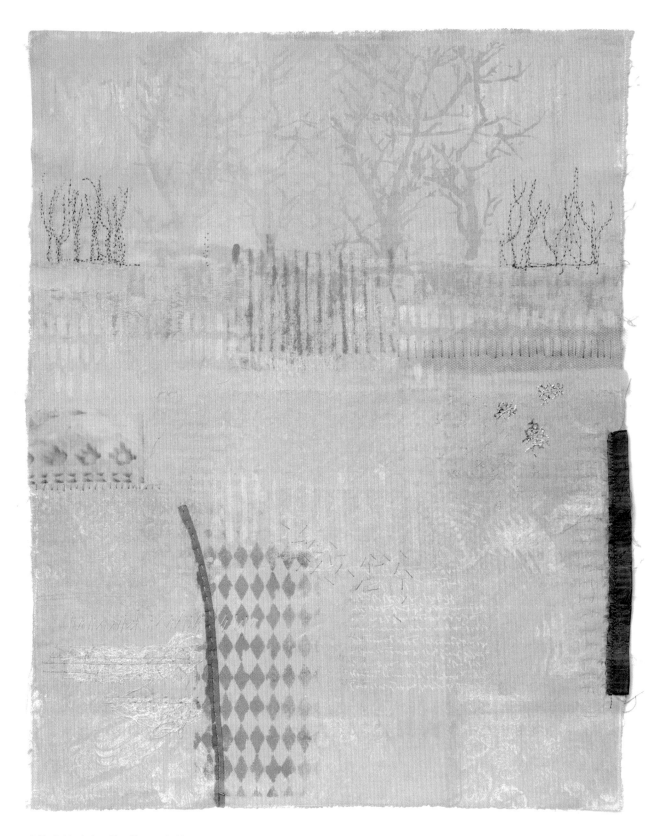

^ My finished piece *One Afternoon in May.*

Printing

When starting a print session, I collect together the things I need – the base fabric, printing plate, roller (brayer), paint, fabric medium, palette knife or old knife to mix paint, mark making tools, and the textures I want to incorporate into the piece. I have favourites that I use again and again, but the list usually includes bubblewrap, corrugated card, scraps of old wallpaper, old lace, leaves or grasses, grids – anything that creates the patterns and textures I'm looking for. I use medium-weight white cotton fabric as it needs to be robust enough to take the layers of acrylic paint and then any stitch or fabric you add later.

Normally, when mono-printing, you would lay the paper onto your printing plate. However, when using fabric, I often leave the fabric on the table and manipulate the plate. I find it helps to have some idea of a colour scheme before I start. It definitely makes your work more personal to be inspired by a photograph you have taken or found, and an observed range of colours from a coastal or woodland walk, your garden, or perhaps seasonal colours.

1. When I'm ready to start, I choose my first colours and mix them with a few drops of fabric medium on the printing plate. It is possible to mono-print on fabric without fabric medium but I find it makes subsequent stitching harder. A few drops of the medium, which is translucent so doesn't affect the colour, mixed into the acrylic paint with a palette knife, allows the fabric to retain a pliability and softness that makes stitching more pleasant. I should add here that I am not trying to have an exact colour match every time I print onto the fabric. In fact, it makes the finished piece more interesting if there are slight variations across the fabric.

2. I used Phthalo Turquoise and white as my first colour and, after rolling out the paint on my printing plate, I made marks into the colour with an old store card and printed them onto the fabric. I don't want to exactly replicate the marks; it's more important to make a range of similar marks and to view them across the whole fabric. I don't add paint every time but judge how much is needed as I progress and any variation in the colour will be adapted as we continue with subsequent layers.

3. After the fabric is printed with the first colour, the shape of the printing plate is quite obvious but subsequent printing will soften that. To blend out the printing plate shape, I tend not to print exactly on top of the first layer. Always view the effect over the full width of fabric rather than the prints as individual marks.

4. For the second colour layer, I gave the paint a slightly grey tone by adding a little duck-egg blue acrylic, giving me a middle range of softer tones. After making different marks for this second layer of printing, some of the first layer will still show through but it is working to create a textured fabric.

5. Pale Olive Green, one of my current favourites, was introduced for the third layer. When mixed with a small amount of white, a range of yellow/green shades can be achieved that will give this project the landscape-inspired colour scheme I want. Whilst printing, I was thinking about a bluebell wood and Pale Olive Green gave me the range of tones we see under a tree canopy at bluebell time, when the sun cuts through the branches. I don't restrict the mixing to two colours at a time but vary the shades by mixing in a touch of turquoise or other blues. Observe the tones within your inspiration image – what colours are in the shadows?

6. As well as making marks on the printing plate, this time I used direct printing for some areas. I used the plate as an inking surface, pressed some surfaces on it and printed them onto the fabric. Two surfaces I often have handy at this stage are corrugated cardboard, which gives a linear pattern, and a textured surface such as bubblewrap to add a circular shape. By this point, I usually have enough paint on the fabric so that nearly all the background fabric has been covered and the shape of the printing plate has all but disappeared. I continue to add colour until I am happy with how it looks.

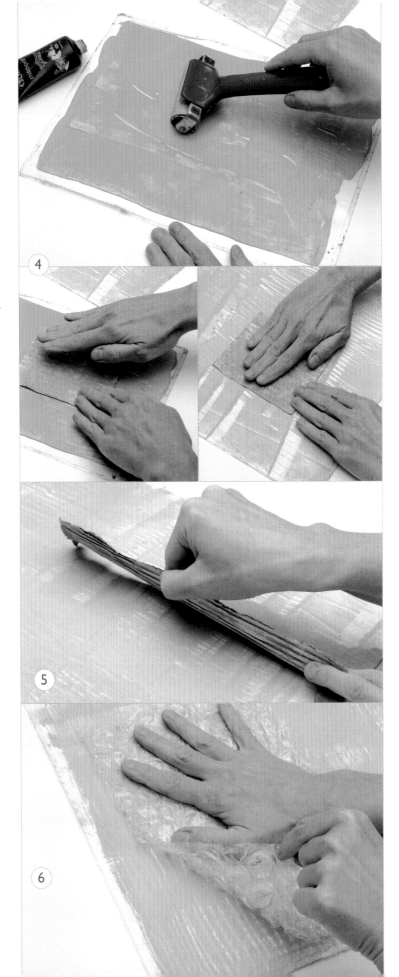

7. Next, I start to add elements in other ways through the use of stencils, screens and collagraph. There are several ways of adding detail at this stage and one, when the paint has dried, is to rub small areas of the fabric surface with an oil pastel to catch the textures underneath. I have sometimes used an old Indian woodblock to add a little bit of pattern, or a manufactured grid. It's not necessary to use the whole of the textured surface – just as much as you need to add the detail you want. You can also lay out your work table elements like grasses, leaves, netting or lace – whatever gives you the texture you need – and add more clearly defined shapes and textures that way.

8. At this stage, I use stencils and screens to surface-print details, perhaps some script or other design detail. Again, it isn't necessary to use the whole screen. However, it has to become a cohesive design and any pattern detail you add must fit in with your overall aim. By this time I have also achieved the intended colour scheme with small areas of complementary colour that highlight the overall design.

9. When the painted surface is completely dry, I always iron the fabric, starting with the back. I use a piece of paper or kitchen roll when I turn it over to iron the painted side. My printed pieces usually have a narrative and after the printing is complete, I use heat bonding web to secure small pieces of fabric, often sheers or silk, to add highlight details within the composition of the piece.

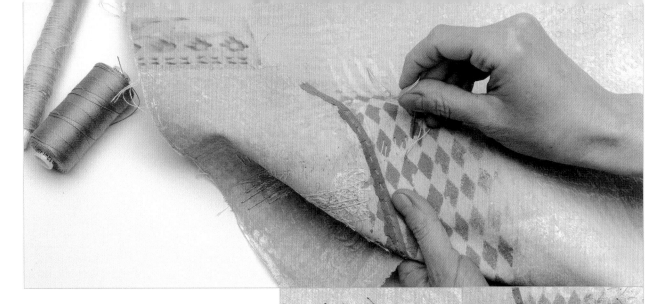

Adding stitch

When I feel I have added all the printed pattern and fabric that is necessary and I'm happy with the design, I add stitch both by machine and hand. The stitch adds coloured marks for an extra highlight. They should be part of the surface to bring a change of scale so I stitch as much as I feel necessary. Anything added at this stage is determined by the theme of the panel.

After another iron to ease out any wrinkles from the stitching, the piece is ready to be used.

Taking it further

There are many uses for printed pieces like these. I often stretch the whole finished stitched print over a bought canvas but I have also cut the print into smaller areas to make a textile book. The composition changes quite dramatically when this is done and can create really interesting pages – be brave!

I have also used sections to make a removable cover for a bought sketchbook and further embellished it by adding other bits of fabric, if needed. I've cut bird shapes, heart shapes and made hanging decorations. I made covered padded buttons as a feature detail for a garment and by ironing areas onto an adhesive such as S80 Vilene, I have made ribboned badges for class groups.

Small pieces of the print can be used as collage with other stitched textile pieces. It is a very useful technique and whatever you do can add a change of scale and detail to other textile work.

Go for it!

CURLING UP WITH A GOOD BOOK
Concertina books and scrolls

Suzette Smart

I love to create textile books and scrolls. Many begin life as mixed media and stitching samples in workshops, which may be finished when I reach home but sometimes remain incomplete to show the layers that make up a piece. They are all different and they evolve alongside my stitching style and inspiration. They become as familiar as old friends as I dip into them for ideas and they travel with me to workshops, talks and sometimes on holiday as I can never go without a needle and thread!

However, they wouldn't be complete without the addition of a cover – which is always an excuse for play. This might be a collage of repurposed embroidery bits I have taken from my boxes or an altogether new page. For this workshop we're going to design and stitch a new book cover to keep all those samples and favourite pieces safe. Don't worry if you change your mind halfway through and your book cover turns into a panel to hang or frame.

For this workshop, I've taken a little bit of inspiration from my *Rose Queen* embroidery. It became a collage of ideas, fabric and mixed media which I developed, adding personal pieces of lace and vintage fabric.

To make my book, I painted four pieces of Bondaweb (fusible webbing) with ditsy flowers, foliage and large and small roses (leaving the paper backing on the Bondaweb). I've added gifted lace, chintz-style fabric roses and a piece of vintage tablecloth as a backing for my bird. I don't have any set way of creating a bird within a piece of work. They are a mix of outline, fabric collage and machine and hand stitched marks. In this workshop, the bird will be created with machine embroidery and fabric collage but you can always add more details with hand stitching.

MATERIALS AND EQUIPMENT

- Two pieces of calico each 16½ × 10½in (42 × 27cm approx)
- Bondaweb (fusible webbing) 10 × 10in (25 × 25cm)
- Acrylic paints (I buy inexpensive sets of acrylics)
- Small paintbrushes – I've used a flat and a round brush
- Fabric with large chintz-style flowers for cutting up
- Baking paper
- Lace
- Fabric for your bird – I used one with a small pattern
- White fabric to go behind bird collage, 5½ × 6½in (14 × 17cm) – a crisp white piece of vintage table linen is lovely for this
- Bird template – to fit onto the white piece of fabric
- Sewing machine with free motion/darning foot
- Suggested threads: dark but not black, an off-white, yellow (you might want to pick a couple more for highlights, and a subtle variegated can be lovely too)

> My completed
  book cover.

Preparing and painting the Bondaweb

The painted Bondaweb is collaged together for the background before adding machine stitch.

1. Prepare the Bondaweb by cutting it up into four or five various sized pieces.

2. With the rough/adhesive side facing up, use masking tape to secure each corner onto the table where you are working.

3. Mix a little of each paint with water until you have a mix (like a watercolour wash) that you can use easily on the Bondaweb. Try it out on a spare piece of Bondaweb first; as the paint dries, it should separate and create texture.

4. Start painting using darker and lighter shades of red for your roses (small and large), and darker and lighter shades of green for the leaves. I used a vibrant yellow for the centre of the small daisy-like flowers.

5. Make your roses by using the darker colour first. Paint a wavy line starting from the centre and working out for the larger flowers, and a smaller version for the small roses. Add some of the lighter shades and leave some areas free of paint for highlights. Add some dabs of green around the smaller roses and paint in leaves for the larger ones.

6. Outline your leaf shapes with the darker green first and then loosely fill in with the lighter shade. I dabbed a little bit of the rose petal colour in between the leaves too.

7. For the daisy-like flowers, randomly dab the yellow paint around your Bondaweb for the flower centres. Add petals with a flat brush. There is no need to put petals on every flower. Try painting the petals of three or four flowers in a darker shade.

8. Don't paint every bit of the Bondaweb but leave clear areas in between the flowers and for highlights on the petals.

9. Only use the painted Bondaweb when it is completely dry. You can speed up the process with a hairdryer (make sure it doesn't get too hot).

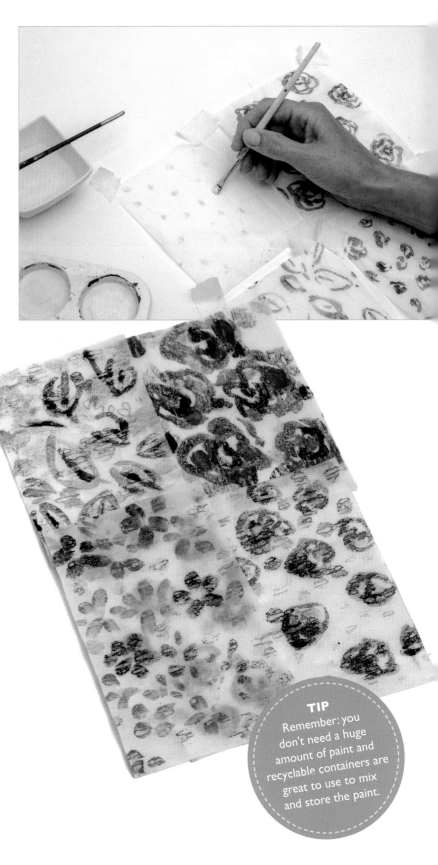

TIP
Remember: you don't need a huge amount of paint and recyclable containers are great to use to mix and store the paint.

Background collage

1. From your materials list, take the lace, white table linen, and cut-out chintz-style flowers, and place them on one side of you, with the painted Bondaweb pieces on the other. Place the calico directly in front of you.

2. Have a play with fitting all the pieces on the calico to create a composition you're pleased with. You may wish to cut some of your painted Bondaweb pieces smaller.

3. When you are happy with your composition, turn the Bondaweb over and pin it in place (adhesive side down). Remove the lace, white fabric and chintzy flowers and put to one side.

4. Take your work to the ironing board. Carefully remove the pins and place a piece of baking parchment over the top to protect your iron. Press firmly as you iron the Bondaweb into place. Check to make sure that the pieces are sticking and adjust the iron temperature accordingly. Remove the baking paper and allow your work to cool before removing the backing paper from the Bondaweb.

5. Place the backing piece of calico behind your work and pin the lace, chintz-style flowers and any other bits you are using in place, catching in the backing as you do so. Your front cover is now starting to take shape.

Drawing your bird

To create my bird, I start with a very simple template drawn on baking paper. You can use the discarded Bondaweb backing paper. Don't worry if you feel you aren't good at drawing – it's the fabrics and stitching that give the bird its character.

I've chosen a fabric with a small print and a piece of vintage lace for my bird which I will cut to size after I've stitched the outline.

When cutting out your bird template, leave a border around the drawn line. Pin your template into place securely.

We're now ready to begin stitching.

TIP
If the paint comes away a little as you are peeling off the backing paper, put it back down and iron again. Remember to let it cool before trying again.

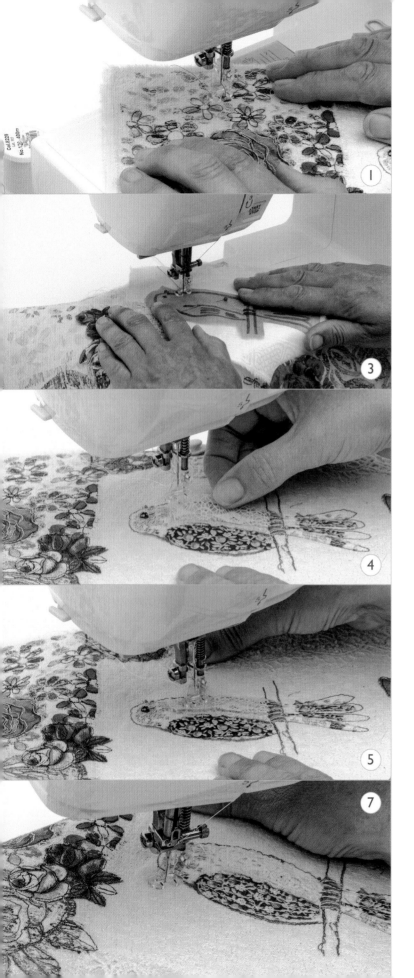

Stitching

Prepare your sewing machine by putting the feed dogs down, the free motion/darning foot on and set for running stitch. Check it is stitching correctly before you begin, by working on some doubled-up fabric. Have your chosen threads at the ready.

Always bring the bobbin thread up to the top before you start stitching to prevent snagging at the back of your work.

If you're new to free machining, it's a good idea to have your manual at hand and to practise on spare fabric.

I have chosen the same dark thread to draw into all the roses, foliage, ditsy flowers and for the outline of the bird. You might prefer another dark colour but I would suggest you don't use black.

1. Follow the wavy lines of your roses to accentuate their blousy shape. It might be easier to work from the centre outwards. Loosely work some of the leaves at the same time.

2. As you stitch the outline of the leaves, remember: it's fine if you want to go outside the lines! Pick out a few of your ditsy flowers to highlight with a stitched outline too.

3. For your bird, follow the drawn lines on your template and when you've finished, carefully pull the paper away.

4. Take your bird fabric with the small print and cut it to fit inside your stitched line, and pin. Cut some of the lace for his tummy and pin. Change your thread for a cream and loosely stitch over the lace and in the direction of the bird's feathers on the small-print fabric. Stitch its eye with the machine or with a French knot.

5. Use cream thread to loosely stitch over the edges of your other pinned lace, to secure.

6. Using a yellow thread, stitch around and around in a small circle for your ditsy flower centres. Do not cut the thread in between but lift the needle and put it down at the next flower. Cut the loose threads when you have finished.

7. Use the same cream thread and loosely stitch in between the flowers and onto the piece of fabric behind the bird, too. Vermicelli-style stitching works well for this and blends the lace and all the fabrics and flowers together.

To finish

You may wish to add an additional piece of ribbon or fabric down the long side and back your book cover with calico or a vintage fabric before stitching it into the seam.

Of course, there is always room for a little hand stitching too!

You can use this process to create many different books and scrolls.

One book I make has a more traditional feel, with a seam on one side and pages you can flip. When I have enough workshop samples or pieces that might one day be framed, I line them up and bind them together with a running stitch up the seam to keep them safe and orderly.

To make a scroll, you could use a vintage bobbin or a piece of dowel for your work to be wrapped around. Cut a piece of calico to the required width/length and then make your mixed media collage. Add a backing material before you begin free machining.

∨ A book or scroll is a perfect project to take on holiday as most fold to a packable size and can double-up as a needle case.

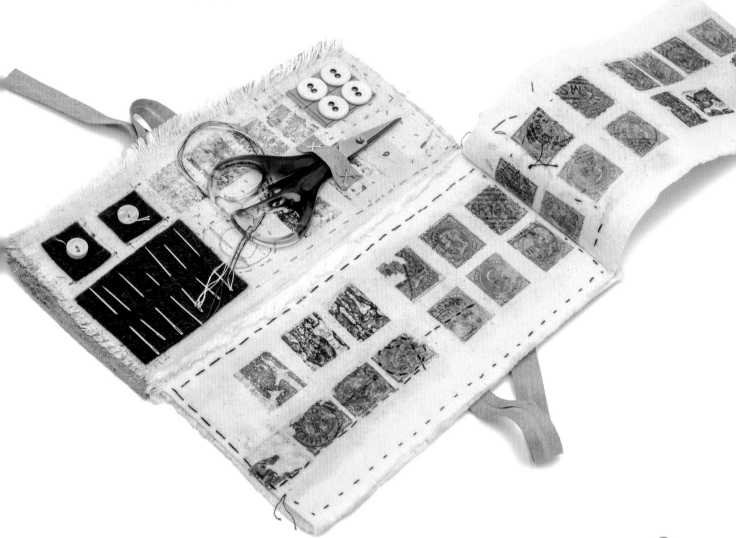

∧ To make these books, I used a vintage pillowcase for the foundation layers and included paper, lace and gifted fabrics in my collage. There is mostly free machine stitching with a little hand stitching detail.

∧ Washes of fabric dyes applied in a painterly fashion, fabric collage and free machine and hand stitching were used for this scroll. It has been loosely wound around a piece of wooden dowel.

∨ I made this book to keep workshop samples safe and in one place.

ARTY APPLICATIONS
Using digital apps to create artwork

Ros Varrie

My husband James and I sold our family home of 38 years in February 2020 and moved into a one-bedroom flat for three weeks, until our new cottage was ready – or so we thought!

The first lockdown happened four days later and we were stranded. We had three suitcases and all our other belongings had been put into storage. James had to work from the bedroom, I had to get out of bed early in the mornings so that he could put up a table, taking it down at the end of the day so that we could get into bed at night. Not an ideal situation, but we managed.

I have a studio in the Harbour Gallery in St Aubin, Jersey, Channel Islands, and all my materials were locked down in there and out of reach. Having no art materials was like cutting off my right arm. However, I did have my phone, an iPad and a printer. I started to play around with photo apps available on my phone and iPad – and loved the results.

As you may have guessed, due to the lockdown, three weeks turned into five months. We finally moved into our new cottage in July 2020.

I thought I would try to give you some ideas of what can be done with these tools, combining them to achieve artistic results for sketchbooks or to produce a finished piece.

NOTE

The directions given in this workshop work on Apple devices such as the iPhone and iPad. The Color Pop Efects Photo Editor app is also available through the Play Store for Android mobile phones and tablets – but they differ slightly from the instructions given here.

∧ The original photo of peonies taken by my friend, Claire Barthorpe, a florist.

^ *Peonies*, my finished
piece.

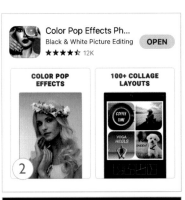

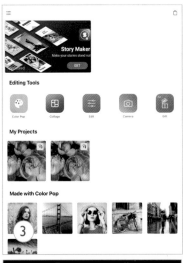

Using Color Pop Effects Photo Editor

1. Select a photo from your library. I screen-shot the photo so it was the last photo taken in the library. Alternatively, create an album for the project.

2. Upload Color Pop Effects Photo Editor from your App Store. The app will want you to subscribe but I recommend that you do NOT do this at this stage.

3. Scroll left until you see an 'X' in the top right corner, then click on it.

4. A new screen appears. Click on 'Color Pop' – it will take a few seconds to load.

5. Now you are in your photo gallery. Click on the image you want to use for this project.

6. You can now choose the size of your photo. I kept mine at its original size. Click on the tick in the top right corner. An advertisement may pop up but just click the 'X' to close it.

7. The image will now be in greyscale. Along the top there is a paintbrush icon, an undo icon and a re-do arrow.

8. Click on the paintbrush icon. Adjust your brush size (I used small to start with) and adjust opacity. Tap the screen to remove the slider.

9. Using your finger, or an Apple Pencil, outline the image you want to colour, then fill it in. The eye button in the top right lets you see the original image which is useful for fine tuning. Save the image to your library.

10. Download the Oilist app from the App Store. This costs £3.49 to buy, but I think it's worth it for the results achieved.

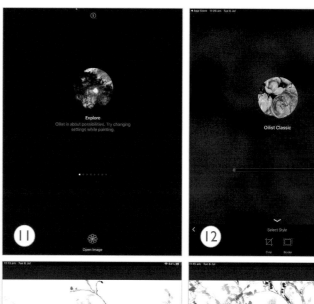

11. Once the app has loaded, open the image you saved in the library from Color Pop.

12. Select a filter (I chose 'Kandinsky Life' for my photograph) and choose one of the three options. Now play around with it. There is a plus sign that blinks. You can take a snapshot as it paints.

13. To keep things simple, I let the app do the work. However, there are many options you can use to achieve some amazing effects.

14. When the painting has finished, you can 'Capture and Finish', or continue playing.

15. I used the Color Pop app first as I wanted the background to be a different colour from my original peach peony. In Oilist, I used the 'Kandinsky Life' filter, as I like the effect.

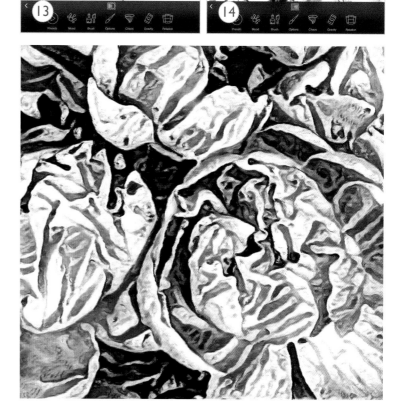

> My finished art in Oilist.

Back to my lockdown story – what happened next?

You remember that all I had in the apartment were a printer, a cotton sheet, an iPad and some A4 sticky labels. This is what I did next.

1. I enhanced the colour in the photo settings on my iPad, as I know that when printing onto fabric and using an inkjet printer, the colour needs bumping up a bit. I then increased the size to 7 x 7in (17.5 x 17.5 cm).

2. I attached the fabric to the A4 sticker and put it through the printer on the highest-quality setting.

3. The results achieved on my cotton sheet were not to my liking – it was too flat – so I sent off for some Dupion silk.

4. I liked the result much better on the silk, as visually it had far more texture and looked 'William Morris' in style.

5. I'm a stitcher so I decided to add some hand embroidery on the main flower.

6. I outlined the dark peach peony using a Frixion pen and used the original photograph to help me sketch the lines.

7. A simple back stitch in three strands of peach-coloured thread was used for the flower petals. I followed the Frixion pen lines to create a slightly raised line. In the centre of the flower, I used loop stitches with yellow thread, which I then cut to represent stamens.

8. When the piece was finished, it was ironed to remove the Frixion pen lines.

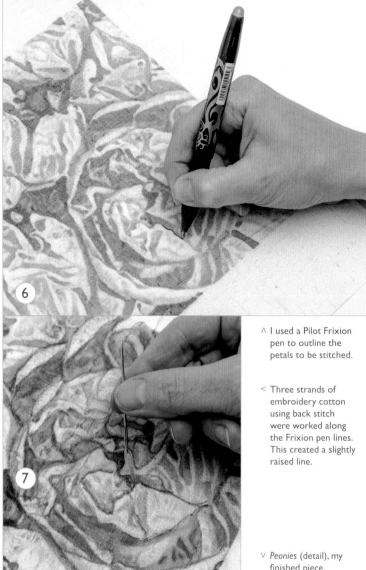

6

7

∧ I used a Pilot Frixion pen to outline the petals to be stitched.

< Three strands of embroidery cotton using back stitch were worked along the Frixion pen lines. This created a slightly raised line.

∨ *Peonies* (detail), my finished piece.

What next?

I was so happy with the result that I used
the design for gifts. I found the website
www.bagsoflove.co.uk. It has so many amazing
items onto which you can have your designs
printed. I now use it for my all fabric printing. The
Bags of Love designing tool is very user-friendly
and you can create to your heart's content.
During lockdown, I had cushions, passport covers,
mugs, aprons and even cufflinks made
using this design.

Many textile artists are using
digital design to enhance
and create interesting fabrics,
which are then worked into
further with other media and
stitch. Our own Maggie Grey is a
master with the computer and her
book *From Image to Stitch* has many
wonderful ideas.

I have really enjoyed discovering apps, as
you can start creating art on the train, bus, in
the doctor's waiting room, on a long journey, or
even in your lunch break.

Have fun discovering and playing with art apps,
taking them off your iPad or tablet and into the
textile world.

∧> I discovered the website *www.bagsoflove.co.uk* and
    used its designing tool to create gifts for family and
    friends using my *Peonies* artwork.

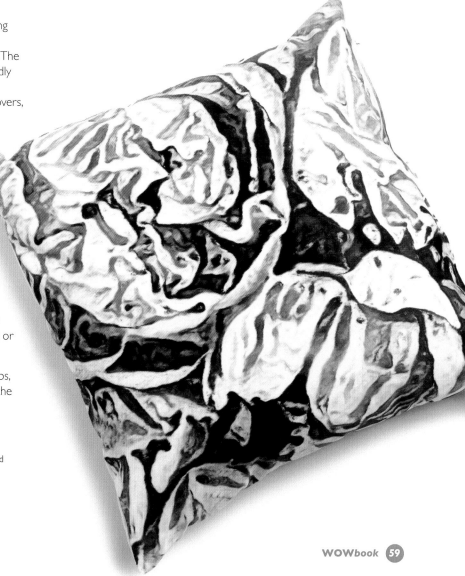

Bev Caleno

I took City & Guilds in Soft Furnishing and Interior Design when my children were very young (I won't say how long ago!). I then ran my own interior design business for several years. With a never-ending supply of samples and offcuts, I started making appliqué cushions and little folksy pictures on curtain buckram using machine embroidery. I also took a qualification in adult education and started running my own workshops and classes.

I live in an old Edwardian bank on the north Essex coast, UK, with my husband who is a plein air painter, and Banksy the dog (a Schnoodle). Our accommodation is above the commercial premises. This consists of a large banking hall and other offices and rooms, including a kitchen in the vault! There is one large studio and three smaller ones, including a textile room with a large cutting table and sewing machines. We run a programme of workshops throughout the year in painting, craft and textiles. We engage some of the top tutors and artists, from whom I have learnt so much. These days, I try to limit myself to textiles and watercolour painting. I draw, stitch or paint nearly every day and have recently started taking my paints out with me, and working *in situ*.

Teaching textile art and machine embroidery is my passion. I enjoy meeting people from different backgrounds and watching them grow in confidence in my classes. I have exchanged many stories of how creative endeavours have seen us all through difficult times.

> *Hippocampus and Hippocampus Croceus.* Each 8 x 8in (20 x 20cm). These are the latest examples for my weekend workshops, using a sample produced by Lynda Monk as the background (thank you Lynda). These were layered using different mixed-media techniques including stitch, print and water-soluble fabric.

I never get bored of stitching, burning, melting and dissolving, and I get very excited about new materials and happy accidents. I love colour and have learnt the power of observation. One day I may be examining the minutiae of a tiny underwater creature and trying to recreate it in textiles, the next, splashing paint around to make a loose representation of a bee or a hare. All of my work is inspired by nature and the environment. I love wildlife and travel.

I count myself lucky to have travelled widely and visited many different countries. I am a reluctant scuba diver – a Professional Association of Diving Instructors (PADI) open water diver – and have completed about 90 dives around the world. My underwater adventures are reflected in my work – there is a whole new world under the sea. My inspiration also comes from exploring nature on my doorstep in the UK. I collect specimens on my walks and work from an endless supply of photographs.

I sometimes feel cheated that I didn't go to art school but I have attended many workshops and classes and spend a lot of time adapting what I have learnt to achieve different outcomes.

I am a member of Colchester Art Society and on the committee of the local embroiderers group. Every year in August, we host our own exhibition where we sell our work and exhibit items made by my textile art group.

www.oldbankstudios.co.uk
Instagram: @old_bank_studios_harwich
www.facebook.com/TheOldBankWorkshops

∨ *Think Tank.* This piece was devised during lockdown, inspired by my many experiences as a scuba diver. It is a 360° Perspex cube sculpture, 15¾ x 15¾in (40 x 40cm). All the creatures here are true to size and colour. I call them 'Textidermy'! This is my entry into Colchester Art Society's winter exhibition.

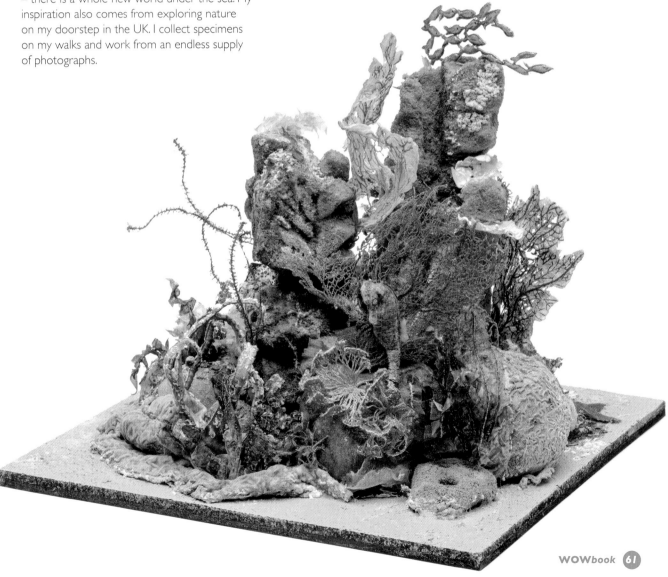

Fran Holmes

I've been creative all my life, which I think stems from my mother and grandmother who were both very creative. My earliest memory of sewing was when my grandmother bought me a squirrel sewing kit when I was eight years old. At primary school in Lincolnshire, UK, sewing was my favourite lesson of the week.

After leaving school, my professional career took me into nursing and midwifery, ending as a health visitor. However, throughout my working life I continued being creative, taking courses in flower arranging and Fabergé egg craft. My creative life really changed when I took two City & Guilds courses with textile artist, embroiderer and tutor, Cherrilyn Tyler. The first was a City & Guilds Level 3 Diploma in Machine Embroidery, and the second was a Level 3 Diploma in Creative Techniques in Textiles.

The college I attended would exhibit annually at the NEC in Birmingham, UK, and this experience gave me a taste for exhibiting my work. Exhibiting gave me the opportunity to meet like-minded people and share ideas. Over the past 10 years, I have exhibited at the NEC, Excel London, the West Country Quilt Show and The Big Textile Show as well as other galleries around the UK including in the Lake District and at Oxford University.

I became hooked on textile art and was fortunate to join two groups that exhibit around the country, Meniscus and Drawn to Stitch, both of which are mentored by Cherrilyn.

< I made this full-sized corset from Lutradur which was stitched in a grid pattern. A design of hanging fuchsias was added using free machine embroidery. Colour was applied to the flowers with sheer fabric.

Over the years, I have found that exhibiting and teaching are something that I really enjoy. I love the challenge that belonging to a group brings, designing from a chosen title theme for a forthcoming exhibition. I also belong to another group, Inspire, which does not exhibit but instead focuses members on teaching and inspiring each other. It's very friendly and everyone brings something to the group with their creativity and original ideas.

Aside from exhibiting, teaching textile art is something I'm very fond of and I have several day schools focusing on machine embroidery techniques, teabag art and serviette quilting, but I am also delighted by the challenge of preparing bespoke textile art day schools and workshops.

I find inspiration for my work from all sorts of places, but especially from trips to art galleries, museums, and my travels. The corsets article written for *WOWbook 08* was inspired by an exhibition on underwear called 'Undressed' at the V&A Museum in London.

My next body of work is called *Paper, Cloth, Stitch*. Stitching into paper is the process I've been developing in recent times. I love the challenge of working with paper and using the results to create something unexpected, like a lampshade, lap quilt, cushions and even a coat.

www.franholmes.com
Instagram: @franholmesarts

> This is a coat made from teabags, which are embellished with tea cups and saucers taken from paper napkins. The coat is edged with black velvet, brown paper, lace, machine-stitched flowers and beads.

< *Sea Urchin 1*.12 x 7in (30 x 18cm). Mixed media, chalks and inks. This drawing was produced as part of a group of studies of sea urchins for future work, developing themes from my recent exhibition 'Memory of Place'. I developed the textural background in a very loose way with acrylic paint and inks, then drew the urchin within the space.

Sheila Mortlock

I have always enjoyed the tactile qualities of fabric and the visual effects of pattern. When I left school, therefore, my choice was to study Printed Textiles and Embroidery at Duncan of Jordanstone College of Art, Dundee (DoJCAD), UK, where I live. My embroidery lecturer, Marion Stewart, had studied under Kathleen Whyte at Glasgow School of Art and she brought to Dundee the ethos that we were artists first and foremost who chose to express ourselves through print and stitch. However, the foundation of it all and how I approach my own teaching practice, was observational drawing.

> *A Long Walk.* Approx. 55in (1.5m). This piece was created using bleached jute, embellished bandage muslin with ink added in places, finished with hand stitch. This was another piece, one of three, that formed part of 'Memory of Place'. The exhibition was all about how a particular landscape can inspire, bring back memories of childhood or, in this case, a long walk. The stitched marks, using mostly linen thread, relate to the sounds heard on the walk.

After gaining my teaching qualification, I taught Art in various secondary schools in Dundee. After some years teaching City & Guilds Stitched Textiles courses and working with HNC/D textile students, I left Dundee FE College in 2012 and became an independent City & Guilds tutor. I now restrict my teaching to day schools and workshops, but have always enjoyed working to help students achieve, sometimes beyond their own expectations.

I was an original member of the textile art group Embryo, formed in 1980 by graduates of DoJCAD as a response to the lack of opportunity for textile artists to exhibit. I participated in nearly every exhibition during the group's 20-year existence. Since its inception, I have been a member of EDGE – Textile Artists Scotland, and was delighted in 2013 to be invited to join the Textile Study Group. I have exhibited with both groups in the UK and in Europe and have a chapter discussing my creative practice in the Textile Study Group's recent publication, *Insights*. Being a member of a group has always been important to me as through the community of like-minded people and their friendship, I believe group membership offers artists the creative support essential for continuing development.

In recent years, the availability to have customised screens made based on my drawings and designs, has allowed me to return to my background in printed textiles, using the print as a foundation. I really enjoy using different processes to develop interesting surfaces as a base for stitch. Over the last two years I have been working on a body of work relating to the boundary areas of the crofting community in Scotland's North West Highlands, examining the liminal areas between cultivated and uncultivated, tamed and wild. The work explores a specific area of the Highlands that has a deep personal meaning for me. As part of the process, all my work has some historical element, and this is no different. I enjoy the information gathering and feel it informs whatever textile work evolves.

In the Spring of 2020, my exhibition 'Memory of Place (a walk in time)' opened in Gairloch Museum, Scotland, UK, and although it was a victim of lockdown, it was well received. I hope to find another venue closer to home to show the work again.

www.sheilamortlock.co.uk

∨ *Gutta Percha.* Three of 15 old golf balls covered with bits from an old wool blanket and embroidered. A buttonholed ring was made as a stand for each ball. Each of the original 15 was created using a different technique. This is another part of my 'Memory of Place' set of pieces and refers to my father's love of golf.

Suzette Smart

I am a textile artist and love to use layers of mixed media, fabric collage and hand and machine stitching in my work. I don't work to a specific formula, which sometimes means that what works one day, doesn't the next. This also means that I always have bits of stitch to hand, ready to be cut up and re-assembled into a jug, tree or maybe a bird. My 2019 large piece, *Draw my World in Words*, used some of these repurposed embroideries and was selected for the inaugural Fine Art Textile Award Gallery at the Festival of Quilts that year.

I studied General Art and Design at the North East Wales Institute of Higher Education (NEWI) in Wrexham, which led to a BA (Hons) in Fashion and Textile Design at The University of Ulster, Belfast from 1990 to 1993. For the last 18 years, I have lived with my family in a rural hamlet in north Shropshire, UK. The Llangollen Canal passes through here and the familiar journeys up and down the towpath and through the fields have become an important source of inspiration for stitching and storytelling. The strong sense of place and belonging are an essential element to my work, along with the birds and animals I find along the way.

The garden birds in my work I often think of as the narrators of the piece. I stick to the birds seen in my garden or nearby, and attach a certain emotion or symbolism to them. I was fortunate to be part of an exhibition at Oriel Ynys Mon on Anglesey in 2017, which celebrated the birds of Wales. One of the pieces included in the exhibition was inspired by a 1952 Rose Queen sash which belonged to my mother. I took the sash, cut it up and reassembled it with other fabrics whilst retaining the shape and text. I was delighted to have made this celebratory piece which has been seen many times and no longer sits in a drawer.

∧ *Draw my World in Words*. 37³⁄₄ x 67³⁄₄in (96 x 172cm). This large piece was selected for the inaugural Fine Art Textile Award Gallery at the Festival of Quilts in 2019. A strong sense of place is an important aspect of my work.

< The inspiration and foundation fabric for this nostalgic piece of work was a 1952 Rose Queen sash belonging to my mother.

∨ The inspiration for this work, *Still Flowering*, is the beautiful cosmos flower, 'Chocamocha', with its dark silhouette. I used a gesso base for the background.

Although I love to blend all the mixed media elements and fabrics that make up a piece with free machine stitching, I also look to emphasise the contrasts and pops of colour. I took this further following eye surgery in Autumn 2020, and began using a soft white gesso base. As I adjusted to a new way of seeing, the strong silhouettes were easier on my eyesight but also inspired new ideas for work. The piece *Still Flowering* was the first of these and was based on the cosmos 'Chocamocha'. This was still in bloom when I was allowed to venture outside.

I'm part of Oswestry Open Studios each June and exhibit both locally and further afield. I deliver talks and workshops throughout the UK, including regular visits to Elm Farm Studio in Essex, and Westhope College and The Willow Gallery in my home county of Shropshire.

www.suzettesmart.com
Instagram: @suzettesmarttextiles

Ros Varrie

I have always loved creating art, with a heavy leaning towards textiles. As a child, my mother taught me to sew by hand, to embroider and to use a sewing machine.

At school, I took Needlework 'A'-level and after leaving school, began training to be a nurse. Due to ill-health, I had to change direction and became a beautician, running my own business.

My three children arrived – two boys and a girl – and as I had a daughter, I started hand-smocking dresses which I made using Liberty Tana lawn. Following that, I took a silk painting class which I thoroughly enjoyed, especially the effects I created; I enjoyed experimenting. A move to Geneva, Switzerland, came next, where I taught silk painting to the ex-pat community.

When we returned to Jersey, the children were grown up and I decided to enrol as a mature student on a full-time Art Foundation course for a year. I really loved my time at college and learnt so many new things such as welding, life drawing, oil painting, working with glass and woodworking.

∧ *Byzantine Portals*. To create this piece, I used textile paints, stencils, wooden blocks and homemade stamps, layering them to create an interesting background. The windows were produced from masks. I machine stitched the windows and columns, adding wool, glass, wire and crystals to the columns. The background was then painted in gold and, finally, I added a ring wrapped with thread, with an old earring attached to it.

> *Mum AKA Betty*. This work was made soon after my mother died. She loved colour and the Swinging '60s. The background was constructed using a Gelli plate with textile paints, gold gilding and machine stitching for the background. The fabric was then collaged, machine stitched and glass black rods wrapped in wire were added. Swarovski crystals finished the piece along with jade elements from one of my mother's necklaces.

Textiles were still my first love but mixed media had begun to creep into my work, and I started experimenting with glass, crystals, wire and stitch. When the course finished, there was a huge empty space in my life – and I missed being with like-minded people.

In Jersey, there is a wonderful gallery, the Harbour Gallery, which was previously run by a retired textile teacher, Di Richardson. She began teaching a two-year 'A'-level Textiles course, so I enrolled and was thrilled to achieve an A* at the end. I am now based at the Harbour Gallery, working out of the loft studio and teaching workshops to adult students. I also help out with textile workshops for adults with learning difficulties, which are held at the gallery. I am constantly amazed at what they all achieve and their work is sold in the gallery, from which they receive a percentage. I was invited to join the Diversity group, which is based at the Gallery. Before Covid, we held an exhibition every year, working to a chosen theme. I believe it is invaluable to attend workshops with other artists, as it broadens my horizons. Currently, I am experimenting with digital technology and ways of incorporating it into my work.

I have developed a range of jewellery using my own designs. I use paper, silk, glass rods, wire and crystals to embellish my pieces and every one is unique. My finished necklaces and pendants are inspired by the Art Deco style.

Photography plays a very important part in my work, inspiring my sketchbooks and finished work. We are very lucky to have such wonderful nature, architecture and coastal scenery in the Channel Islands.

www.rosalindvarrie.com
Instagram: @rosalindvarrie_design

< *Rush Hour.* Hand-painted silk tie.

> Collar necklace. A Gelli plate was used to make the material. Glass rods wrapped in wire and Swarovski crystals were added.

> Pendant necklace. Again, a Gelli plate was used to make the material. This was tweaked in Photoshop and printed out on high-quality paper. I used silk Dupion paint in a co-ordinating colour. Glass rods wrapped in wire and Swarovski crystals were added.